Rebecca Brewton Motte

American Patriot and Successful Rice Planter

1737-1815

Margaret F. Pickett

© 2022 Margaret F. Pickett

All rights reserved. No part of this book may be reproduced or transmitted in any form or by any means, electronic or mechanical, including photocopying, recording, or by any information storage and retrieval system, without permission in writing from the copyright owner.

Pickett, Margaret F. *Rebecca Brewton Motte: American Patriot and Successful Rice Planter*
Published by Evening Post Books, Charleston, South Carolina.

ISBN-13: 978-1-929647-70-5

Cover and interior design by Michael J. Nolan

Cover photo by Fabian Liebermann

Author photo by Kellie McCann

Dedication

To Luther Wannamaker,

The tireless steward of the site of Fort Motte

Table of Contents

Preface and Acknowledgments vii
Map of Places Associated with Rebecca Motte ix
Prologue x

One: The Brewton Family 1
Two: The Motte Family 14
Three: Rebecca and Jacob 22
Four: The Road to Revolution 35
Five: War Comes to the South 50
Six: British Occupation of South Carolina — Part One 62
Seven: British Occupation of South Carolina — Part Two 76
Eight: Fort Motte — Part One 89
Nine: Fort Motte — Part Two 103
Ten: The British Evacuation of South Carolina 119
Eleven: The End of the War and a New Beginning 134
Twelve: The Rice Planter 149

Epilogue 167
Addendum: Fort Motte — Then and Now 170
Chapter Notes 175
Bibliography 190
Index 194

Preface and Acknowledgments

Prior to moving to Bluffton, South Carolina in 2010, I lived in Williamsburg, Virginia, where, in the course of twenty years, I worked for the Jamestown-Yorktown Foundation, and the Colonial Williamsburg Foundation. I also portrayed a person of the past for the National Park Service at Historic Jamestowne. While my knowledge of 17th- and 18th-century Virginia history was quite extensive, I knew little about the colonial history of South Carolina. So I delved into the state's history, as I was intrigued with the story of rice planter Eliza Lucas Pinckney. Since I enjoyed doing "living history" (impersonating a person from the past), I decided to portray this fascinating and remarkable woman. I later wrote *her biography, which was published in 2016*.

I prefer to portray characters that I have thoroughly researched. When Carole and George Summers, organizers of the Francis Marion Symposium, asked me to portray Rebecca Motte that fall, I agreed, even though I knew very little about her. I had only a few months to prepare, did as much research as I could, and put together a program with the story of the Siege of Fort Motte as the centerpiece. At the conclusion, an audience member asked if I would write a biography of Rebecca Motte? I had thought about doing so because, as I did my research on Eliza, I found frequent references to Rebecca and the Motte family. The seed was planted, although little information about Rebecca was available. At a later date, Charles Baxley, editor and publisher of the magazine *Southern Campaigns of the American Revolution*, and Luther Wannamaker, who owns the Fort Motte site, said Rebecca Motte deserved recognition not only for her patriotism during the American Revolution, but also for her business acumen and accomplishments after the war.

I was hooked, and began digging through family correspondence, legal documents, and newspaper articles. Unlike Eliza,

Rebecca left few letters, but there have been various and inconsistent articles written about her. However, Rebecca liked to tell stories about her experiences during the American Revolution, and her descendants had passed them down. Yet when stories are repeated many times, the details become blurred. I searched for kernels of truth and noted them.

The earliest written account of Rebecca's activities during and after the Revolution was in Elizabeth Ellet's *The Women of the American Revolution,* a collection of stories about contributions made to the war by women from each of the thirteen original colonies. The first two volumes of Ellet's three-volume set were published in 1849. Since she had talked to Rebecca's grandchildren and great-grandchildren, her information was likely more accurate than accounts published in the 1870s and early 1900s.

Still, the best sources about Rebecca's life was in *The Papers of Eliza Lucas Pinckney and Harriott Pinckney, Horry Digital Edition,* and *The Papers of the Revolutionary Era Pinckney Statesmen, Digital Edition,* both edited by Constance B. Schulz, distinguished professor emeritus of history at the University of South Carolina, and published by the University of Virginia Rotunda Press. Professor Schulz and her staff did a marvelous job compiling the digital editions. They also added new information. In addition, the papers of the Pinckney family statesmen included details about Rebecca and the Mottes. I also consulted wills, census records, land-sale agreements, lawsuits, newspaper notices, histories, and contemporary memoirs about her. I have had to make assumptions, but also offer the facts that led to them. This allows readers to come to their own conclusions about Rebecca's story.

The primary source material letters, documents, etc. quoted in this book have been modified for modern readers. There was no standard spelling for most of the 18th century; most people spelled words phonetically, often the same word differently in the same paragraph. There were no standards for punctuation and grammar. Many nouns are capitalized in the middle of sentences, and verb usage was not consistent. I have chosen to preserve the original spelling and capitalization as much as possible. Abbreviations such as "wch" for "which" and "ye" for "the," have been written out and elevated letters brought down. Illegible words, words missing from the original document, or an explanation of a word or event are in brackets. Words in parentheses are original to the writer. Most of the punctuation has been preserved with the exception of the frequent run-on sentences that make passages so difficult to read; these are broken up with semi-colons.

Dates are often confusing for the first half of the 18th century because until 1752 the new year began on March 25. Thus, an event that took place in February 1745 would, by our reckoning, have occurred in the year 1746. I have advanced the year of all dates before 1752 to correspond to modern usage.

This book covers a long span of time, and some place names have changed. On August 13, 1783, "Charles Town" officially became "Charleston." For the sake of clarity, I have chosen to use the modern name when referring to the city, except when quoting from primary source documents. Although ruled by the same monarch starting in 1603, England and Scotland were separate countries until 1707 when the Acts of Union was passed. The two countries became Great Britain; however, the terms "English" and "British" were often used interchangeably after this time period.

I could not have written this book without the help and support of many people. I especially thank Luther Wannamaker for his untiring encouragement and support. Dick Watkins helped sort out history of land ownership in the Fort Motte area. Charles Baxley assisted in clarifying 18th-century legal matters; Steven D. Smith, research professor at the University of South Carolina and former director of the South Carolina Institute of Archaeology and Anthropology, conducted the excavations at

Rebecca Brewton Motte

Fort Motte and gave me important insight into the siege; Dr. Walter B. Edgar shared his expertise and I thank my good friend Mary Pinckney for encouragement and for introducing me to many interesting people.

Pierre Manigault gave me a tour of the Miles Brewton House in Charleston — an unforgettable experience. John Oller, fellow scholar and author, shared information with me; Virginia Ellison of the South Carolina Historical Society helped me with my research; Rachel Pickett, my granddaughter, and John Fisher, archaeologist at the South Carolina Institute of Archaeology and Anthropology, created the map; and my son Dwayne was always there to listen, encourage, and exchange ideas.

Prologue

In the late 1840s, Elizabeth Ellet was making a journey from her home in Columbia, South Carolina, to visit the site of a Revolutionary War engagement — the Siege of Fort Motte. At the end of 1845, Mrs. Ellet, already the author of several books, had decided to undertake a new project: publish an account of the hitherto untold stories of the women of the American Revolution. The books, three in number, would be a collection of anecdotes and information about the contributions made to the war effort by women from each of the original colonies. She planned to gather her information from published accounts of the war, letters, diaries, and interviews with descendants of the women.

After reading an account of the Siege of Fort Motte, Mrs. Ellet had been intrigued, for a woman had played a pivotal role in the American capture of the fort. Her name was Rebecca Motte, and in January of 1781, the British had appropriated her plantation, commandeered her house, fortified it to use as a supply depot, and called it Fort Motte. When the Americans arrived to lay siege to the fort, Rebecca had willingly agreed to sacrifice her house to ensure their victory. Since the site of Fort Motte was only thirty or forty miles from her home, Mrs. Ellet decided she must see it for herself.

When she reached her destination, Mrs. Ellet was truly impressed. The fort had been situated on the crest of a high hill on the south side of the Congaree River. She described the view:

> The height commands a beautiful view, several miles in extent, of sloping fields, sprinkled with young pines, and green with broom grass or the corn or the cotton crops; of sheltered valleys and wooded hills, with the dark pine ridge defined against the sky. The steep overlooks the swamp land through which the river flows; and that may be seen to a great distance, winding like a bright thread, between the sombre forests.[1]

The scene now was peaceful, but Mrs. Ellet could picture in her mind what it must have looked like in May of 1781 when the American forces under General Francis Marion and Colonel Henry Lee arrived to lay siege to the fort. She could visualize Marion's men encamped on the grounds to the east and Lee's men four hundred yards to the north, near the house where Rebecca Motte and her female relations had taken refuge. She could imagine the American leaders earnestly explaining to Rebecca that they had to take the fort before British forces arrived, and the relief they must have felt when Rebecca was not only willing for them to set fire to her house, but also provided them with the means of doing so. Mrs. Ellet was in awe: "I have stood upon the spot, and felt that it was indeed classic ground, and consecrated by memories which should thrill the heart of every American,"[2]

Satisfied with her visit, Elizabeth Ellet returned home, making a mental note to contact the descendants of Rebecca Motte and interview them. She was impressed with Rebecca's patriotism, unselfishness, and generosity. She had to find out more about her.

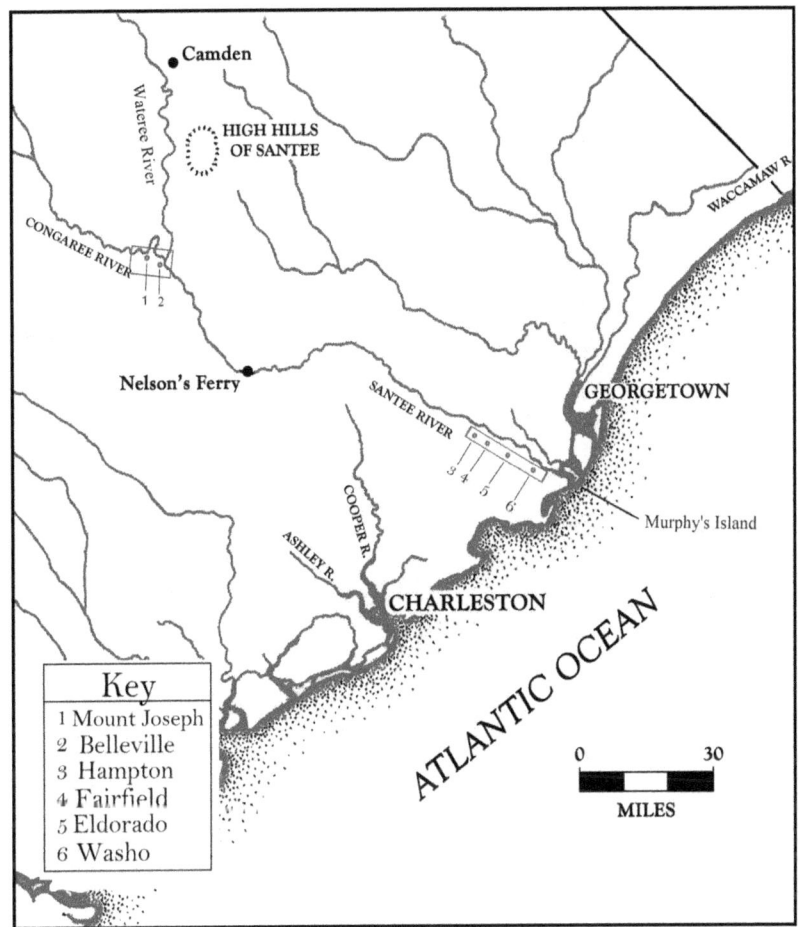

Map created by John Fisher

Chapter One
The Brewton Family

Rebecca Brewton was the fourth of five children born to Robert Brewton and his second wife Mary Griffith Loughton Brewton. On her father's side, Rebecca was a fourth-generation South Carolinian, her paternal great-grandfather having come to the colony in July of 1684 with his wife, nine-year-old son Miles, and daughters Susannah and Elizabeth.[1] It is generally thought the Brewton family came to South Carolina from the island of Barbados, as there is a record of a Robert Bruton, aged eleven arriving in Barbados from Andover, England, in March of 1640.[2] Settled in 1627, Barbados was sparsely populated when Robert arrived, and there were many opportunities for advancement. However, by the 1680s such possibilities had dwindled, and many islanders, like the Brewtons, were leaving to seek their fortunes in the young colony of Carolina.

At this time the Carolina colony was one large province that stretched from the Virginia border to the present border between Georgia and Florida. Charles II had granted this vast territory to eight of his loyal supporters in 1663 and 1665. These eight men were the Lords Proprietors of the colony, responsible for settling, governing, and protecting the province in return for a chance to enhance their private fortunes with plantations in the New World. However, it was not until 1669 that Anthony Ashley Cooper, one of the proprietors, organized an expedition to settle the colony.

In the spring of 1670, the first colonists arrived off the coast of present-day South Carolina and began to look for a place to locate their settlement. The area they eventually chose had a large, natural harbor formed by the confluence of two rivers, which they promptly named the Ashley and the Cooper. The colonists built their first settlement on the west side of the Ashley River, ten miles from its mouth, and called it "Charles Towne" in honor of the king. Ten years later, in 1680, "Charles Towne" was moved across the Ashley River to its present location. Therefore, when the Brewton family arrived in "Charles Towne" in 1684, they found a town in the early stages of development.

Land was readily available in the Carolina colony, and many of the first settlers had turned to agriculture to make their fortunes. They grew corn, raised hogs and cattle to slaughter for salt beef and pork, and exported them to Barbados, where, since the island depended on imports to feed its population, such commodities were in great demand. The exportation of corn and hogs was profitable, but cattle proved more profitable. By the time the Brewtons came to South Carolina, the cattle industry was on its way to becoming the most lucrative economic venture of the 17th century.

However, there was also money to be made in trade with the Native Americans — slaves and deerskins being the two commodities most sought-after by European traders. While the slave trade proved profitable at first, deerskins became more lucrative, continuing well into the 18th century. Trade with Native Americans prospered, and was soon second only to the cattle industry in economic importance. As trade grew in importance it spawned a need for related commercial ventures such as transportation and finance.

Consequently, when the Brewton family arrived in Charleston, they had a choice: take advantage of the generous land grants and raise livestock or establish themselves in the commercial sector. Rebecca's great-grandfather chose the commercial sector. If he had decided to make his fortune in agriculture, his son Miles would have likely followed in his footsteps. However, when Miles Brewton reached adulthood, he did not take up residence on family land in the country, but instead remained in Charleston and established himself as a goldsmith — a 17th- and 18th-century term for a banker.[3] Since there were no banks in South Carolina or in any of the other British colonies, and only one bank — the Bank of England — in London, goldsmiths played an essential role in the economy. Miles had chosen his profession wisely — it was both lucrative and vital.

As Miles was growing up, an elite society had been forming in the South Carolina Lowcountry. Familial connections were at the very heart of it. At first, families sought alliances through marriages with families with whom they were associated. Prosperous planters married their sons and daughters to the daughters and sons of other wealthy planters nearby, while in Charleston the children of successful businessmen married the children of their father's business partners or associates.

Charleston was the center of commerce, the seat of government and learning, the gateway to Europe and the West Indies, and, as the location of the only courts, it was also the legal center for the colony. Every Lowcountry planter, therefore, felt the need to have a house in Charleston and to spend several months of every year there. It was in Charleston, then, that the families of planters met and mingled with those of the successful businessmen and lawyers living in town, and the two groups eventually blended into one large, elite Lowcountry society.

In the 18th century, South Carolina society was fluid; newcomers were always welcome and humble beginnings were no obstacle to membership. It was an open society with wealth as the chief requirement. However, members of this elite society did have obligations. They were expected to serve their colony and take an active role in civic and government affairs.

Following the pattern of the times, Miles Brewton, after establishing himself in the banking business, was ready to take the next step and start a family. Miles would marry three times, and though there are records of his second and third marriages, there is, unfortunately, no existing record of his first marriage and the name of his first wife, the mother of his children, is unknown. Most likely, she was from Charleston and was the daughter of a man who had a business connection with the Brewton family. The two were married sometime before 1698, for in that year, their first child, Robert, was born, followed by five more children — all girls.[4]

By 1709 Miles was important and influential enough in the colony to be chosen captain of one of the two militia units in Charleston, later rising to the rank of colonel. As a further recognition of his standing in the community, on December 7, 1717, the Carolina legislature — the Commons House of Assembly — appointed him Powder Receiver for the province. It was a position he held until his death. As the Powder Receiver, it was his duty to collect a tax from every ship's captain entering a South Carolina port and issue a receipt showing that the tax had been paid. When first levied in 1686, the tax was supposed to be paid in black powder to ensure that an adequate supply of gunpowder was available in case of attack. In 1690 this changed, and the tax was paid monetarily.

By 1717 Miles's son Robert had followed in his father's footsteps and embarked upon a career in the world of commerce and finance. While we know much about Robert's life as an adult, we know almost nothing about his childhood. Although he eventually joined his father in the banking business, it appears he began his career as a merchant and then expanded his commercial interests to include banking.

In 1718 Robert, being well-established in business, was ready to start a family. In either 1718 or early 1719 he married his first wife, Millicent Bullock, the daughter of John and Mary Bullock. Their first child, a boy named Robert, was born on December 17, 1719. He was quickly followed by daughter Mary in 1720 and another daughter Elizabeth in 1724. Sadly, in April of 1728, Millicent Brewton died. One year later on April 15, Robert Brewton married Mrs. Mary Griffith Loughton, a widow with two daughters.[5]

The new Brewton household must have been a lively one consisting as it did of five children: Mary's two daughters: Mary and Anne aged thirteen and seven respectively,[6] and Robert's children: ten-year-old Robert, Mary aged nine, and the five-year-old Elizabeth. The size of the family would soon increase. In January of 1731, Mary gave birth to a son named Miles, and in June of 1733, a daughter named Frances was born. Robert and his expanding family then moved into a house his father had built for him at 71 Church Street in Charleston.[7]

The decade of the 1730s was one of growth and prosperity for South Carolina. In 1719, unhappy with the way the Lords Proprietors had governed the colony, the Commons House of Assembly had asked the king to assume control of the province. In 1721 an interim royal governor arrived in Charleston, and in 1729 South Carolina officially became a royal colony. Newcomers, attracted by the promise of land, religious freedom, and representative government, flocked to the colony. The price of rice soared, and men who had come to Carolina intending to make their fortunes and return to live the good life in England, were suddenly talking about staying.

Just as wealthy planters had felt the need for a house in town, prosperous merchants were now feeling the need for a place in the country, and Robert Brewton was no exception. The place he chose for his country seat was Christ Church Parish (present-day Mt. Pleasant) — a sandy stretch of land lying across the harbor from Charleston. Originally settled by small farmers and tradesmen, the area was now beginning to attract more wealthy inhabitants like merchants William Pinkney and Jacob Motte Sr. Indeed, the fact that Robert's sister Ruth had married William Pinckney in 1725 may have influenced Robert's decision to settle there.

Consequently, sometime between 1734 and 1740, Robert moved his family to his country estate in the parish and, the last three Brewton daughters were likely born there.[8] Rebecca, the middle of the three daughters, was born June 15, 1737. The birthdates of the other two are not known, but Anne, the oldest, was probably born around 1735 and Susannah, the youngest, about 1739.[9] In 1745 Miles Brewton died, and Robert was appointed to succeed his father as the Powder Receiver for the colony. Feeling he needed to be in Charleston to carry out his new duties, Robert moved his family back to town.[10]

Rebecca was born into a world of wealth and privilege. Her father and grandfather were not only prosperous businessmen, but also leaders in the community. Robert was an officer in his militia unit, reaching the rank of colonel like his father before him. He served in the legislature, first representing St. Philip's Parish — the city of Charleston — then representing Christ Church Parish after his move to the country. Robert also held the position of vestryman in both parishes — a position of some importance in the colonial era. The Church of England was the established church in South Carolina and, as such, was an arm of local government. Therefore, vestrymen were government officials who helped the church carry out its public duties.

For three generations, the Brewtons lived, worked, and prospered in South Carolina. Over the years, they developed a deep attachment to the colony and felt an obligation to serve and protect it. Therefore, loyalty and service to colony were highly stressed in the Brewton household.

Rebecca grew up as part of a large blended family. However, her half-brother and half-sisters, being considerably older than she was, did not play a large role in her childhood. Her half-brother Robert was eighteen when she was born and, at some point, left Charleston to live in Bermuda to expand the family's mercantile business.[11] Her half-sister Mary Loughton was married and settled in her own home the year before Rebecca was born, and her other half-sisters were all married by the time Rebecca was five.

Nevertheless, there would have been constant visits between the families, and Rebecca would have been well-acquainted with her half-sisters, their husbands, and their children. Likewise, the Brewton family in Charleston would have been in frequent contact with Robert in Bermuda. Duty to family was an all-important responsibility in the 18th century, and that fact would have been firmly instilled in all the Brewton children at an early age.

By the time Rebecca was five years old, the number of children still living at home had dwindled to five. Since her brother Miles, six years her senior, would have spent most of his time at his lessons or serving his apprenticeship, it was Frances, Anne, and Susannah who were Rebecca's closest childhood companions. The four girls would have engaged in all the normal activities suitable for young ladies at their social level. Outside they would have played tag and battledore (forerunner of badminton), rolled hoops, and chased butterflies in the garden. Inside there were lessons to learn, samplers to stitch, and dolls to dress in the latest fashions. They would have held tea parties for the dolls using miniature porcelain tea sets imported from England — practicing for the day when they, as young women, would preside over the tea table in their own parlors.

Rebecca and her sisters clearly understood the roles they were to play in life. They were to marry, be a wife, mother, mistress of the house, and a helpmate to their male relations — husbands, fathers, and brothers. The Brewton girls all expected to marry wealthy men and have a staff of enslaved servants to do the housework. However, the responsibility for seeing that the household was well-run would rest squarely on their shoulders — the highest accolade for women at this time was to be known as a "notable housewife." To this end Rebecca and her sisters had to learn how to do all the chores they would assign their enslaved servants. Mary Brewton would have made sure that her daughters had all the expertise and knowledge they needed to be known as "notable housewives."

Since playing a musical instrument and being a graceful dancer were considered important for 18th-century girls, Mary probably engaged a music teacher to give her daughters lessons on either the harpsicord or the guitar — two of the instruments considered suitable for ladies. She most likely enrolled them in a dancing class taught by one of the many dancing masters who advertised in the *South Carolina Gazette*. There the girls would have learned the intricate steps of the minuet and the movements in the most popular of the casual country dances.

Girls were also expected to be charming and gracious hostesses in their own homes and to be able to mix well in society outside their homes. Therefore, they needed to learn the social graces: deportment, conversational skills, and manners. With four daughters close in age to educate, Mary may have engaged a governess to teach the girls the social graces along with penmanship, reading, fancy needlework, and basic arithmetic — essential for girls who would one day manage a large household and keep the accounts. What additional lessons the girls received would have depended on what Mary and Robert Brewton thought appropriate for their daughters.

Formal education for girls in the 18th century was a matter of chance, for it depended on the attitude of the father toward education, the economic and social level of the family, and whether the mother was educated or not. There were many fathers who did not place much importance on educating their daughters, even though they could well afford to do so. Housewifery skills, which most girls learned from their mothers, and lessons in deportment, dancing, and music were all that many considered necessary.

However, there were fathers who considered education to be an asset in a woman. A wife was expected to further her husband's interests by being a gracious hostess and mixing well in society. Being a good conversationalist was a valuable social skill. Polite conversation required a light, civil tone with references to current affairs, art, music, and even biblical or classical allusions. Therefore, some knowledge of history, religion, the arts, and the "globes," as geography was called, was helpful.

We do not know how Robert Brewton felt about education for his daughters and, unfortunately, we know very little about Rebecca's mother. Mary was a widow when she married Robert, and in her first husband's will she had been instructed to use the "profits, rents, income both from my real and personal estate for the maintenance, Education, Schooling and Clothing of my said children."[12] It seems, then, that Mary's first husband wanted his daughters to be educated. It may very well be that Mary shared his regard for education and saw to it that the daughters from both her marriages received more than the customary instruction. It is obvious from Rebecca's few surviving letters that she received some formal education, for her handwriting is well-formed and flowing, her spelling is consistent, and she expresses herself well.

Whatever constituted Rebecca's formal education, she also had the advantage of growing up in a household that offered her opportunities to enhance her knowledge of the world. There were books and maps to peruse in Robert Brewton's library. Guests at the Brewton house included the families of the most influential business and political leaders in South Carolina. What stimulating and interesting conversations must have taken place at the dining table and afterwards in the drawing room at the

Brewton house. The young Rebecca listening to these conversations would have gained an insight into the business and political worlds of 18th-Century Charleston.

In 1750, when Rebecca was thirteen years old, tragedy struck the Brewton family. In October her older sister Anne, who could not have been more than fifteen years of age, died.[13] There are no details concerning her death, but she died and was buried October 10, 1750. Her death would have been a crushing blow for the entire family, but it must have been especially devastating for the three remaining sisters. Anne's passing was a poignant reminder of the uncertainty of life in the 18th century.

After mourning their sister's death, the three girls slowly returned to their usual activities. For Frances, that meant a return to the Charleston social scene. While marriage would have certainly been at the back of her mind, at eighteen, she would have been in no particular hurry to find a husband — twenty or twenty-one being the average age for an upper-class 18th-century girl to marry. After all, the teenage years were supposed to be a period of carefree enjoyment for young women. It was felt they deserved this respite, for when they married, they would face a lifetime of duties and responsibilities, not to mention the prospect of childbearing with all its attendant dangers.

By 1752 Rebecca was ready to enter society and accompany her older sister to parties and balls. As she did so, she could not have helped noticing that Frances was spending more and more time in the company of their first cousin Charles Pinckney II — the son of William Pinckney and Ruth Brewton Pinckney. Charles, who had been named after his uncle, Charles Pinckney, had gone to live with him and his first wife Elizabeth Lamb Pinckney when he was ten years old. When he was fourteen, his uncle had sent Charles off to London to complete his education. Now at twenty-three, Charles was a promising young lawyer, ready to marry and start a family. The attraction between Frances and Charles was mutual, and the couple was married on January 2, 1753.

With Frances married and established in her own household, there were just Rebecca and Susannah left at home. While Susannah, at thirteen, may not have been old enough to participate in the social season in 1753, she would, at least, have joined Rebecca for the 1755 season. What fun the two girls must have had going to parties and balls together and then coming home to exchange gossip, comment on the latest fashions, and compare notes on the young gentlemen they found attractive. It would have been a happy, carefree time for both of them.

Then it all ended. In the late summer of 1755, tragedy struck the Brewton family once again. On September 4, Susannah died. Her obituary, which appeared in the *South Carolina Gazette*, does not mention an accident or a lingering illness, therefore, Susannah may have died suddenly — not unheard of in the 18th century when a cut or scratch could become infected with fatal results. Her obituary simply states: "On Monday last died, Miss *Susannah Brewton*, a young Lady whose Death is truly lamented by all that knew her, as she was possessed of all those qualifications that render her respectable."[14]

Rebecca was only eighteen years old and she had lost the two sisters closest to her in age — her childhood companions and confidantes. She must have been shattered. At least when Anne died, Frances and Susannah had been there to share the pain and sorrow with her. Now she was alone — there were no siblings close at hand to comfort her. However, Rebecca was resilient, and just as she had learned to live with the loss of one sister, she would now learn to live with the loss of another. Perhaps the deaths of close family members at a young age helped prepare her for future losses — Rebecca would outlive all her siblings, her husband, four of her six children, and one of her grandchildren.

As a grown woman, Rebecca was petite. Later in life, one of her great-granddaughters left this description of her:

> She was rather under-sized and slender, with a pale face, blue eyes, and grey hair that curled slightly under a high crowned ruffled cap. She always wore a square white neckerchief pinned down in front, tight sleeves reaching only to the elbow, with black silk mittens on her hands and arms; a full skirt with huge pockets, and at her waist a silver chain, from which hung her pin-cushion and scissors and a peculiarly bright bunch of keys.[15]

What Rebecca lacked in inches, however, she made up for in vitality. Lively and energetic, she was a firm believer in the efficacy of leading an active and busy life, doing her best to instill these traits in her children and even her grandchildren. She once wrote to her daughter Mary Alston, "tell B (Mary's daughter) I am sorry to hear she is so lazy and indolent; you must let her come and stay with me the winter and I will endeavor to make her more active."[16] Rebecca must have been successful, for, according to family legend, B (Rebecca Brewton Alston) grew up to be "remarkable for energy and diligence as well as amiability."[17]

Rebecca was well known during her lifetime for her kindness and generosity. Eliza Pinckney once described her as a woman with "a goodness of heart, which has always influenced her to assist all within her reach."[18] And her reach was wide — the recipients of her kindness even included enemy soldiers during the War for American Independence. There was one British officer who was so grateful for Rebecca's kind attention to him that he took advantage of a chance encounter to repay her kindness ten years after the end of the war.

The officer, or most likely, former officer, was said to be perusing the shelves of a book stall in London in 1793 or 94 when he noticed a handsome set of books — a Pulpit Bible, Prayer Book, and Book of Instructions. He was startled when he opened one of the books and saw a name that he recognized inscribed on the inside cover. In 1768 Jacob Motte had commissioned the building of a Parish Church in St. James Santee and Rebecca had presented the church with the three books inscribed with her name. Unfortunately, they had been plundered from the church by the British during the war. The man promptly purchased the books and turned them over to the American minister in London — who happened to be Thomas Pinckney, Rebecca's son-in-law. They were subsequently returned to St. James Santee.[19]

However, anyone who viewed the diminutive Rebecca with her kind and courteous nature as a meek and frail person had made a grave error. Underneath her benevolence and graciousness there lay a will of iron. Rebecca was not a person to shrink from life's challenges, but would meet them head on with resolve and persistence. Perhaps this was a trait she learned by observing how her mother and other female relations faced life's trials, or perhaps it sprang from her own experience in dealing with the loss of her sisters. It may just have been inherent in her nature. Perhaps it was a combination of all three. Wherever it came from, or however she attained it — Rebecca had grit.

When she finished grieving for her sister, Rebecca was ready to resume her social life and begin to look for a suitable husband. At nineteen she was well-prepared for the next phase of her life. She had received a better than average education and, in the future, would prove to as competent at managing a plantation as she was at managing a household. She had charming manners and later won praise for her gracious hospitality — some of it rendered under trying circumstances. She was also known for her conversational skills. Her contemporaries said that she conversed "with ease, vivacity and good sense."[20] Rebecca had been on the social scene now for several years and had had the opportunity to meet many eligible young men, but there was one who stood out from all the rest. His name was Jacob Motte Jr.

Chapter Two
The Motte Family

Jacob Motte Jr. was the eldest son of Jacob Motte Sr. and his first wife Elizabeth Martin Motte. The Motte family originally came from France. The Marquis de la Motte, Jacob's great-grandfather, and his wife and children were among the many French Protestants or Huguenots who fled France in 1685 when Louis XIV revoked the Edict of Nantes, thereby depriving them of their religious and civil liberties. While many Huguenots immigrated to England or the British colonies in North America, some, like the Marquis de la Motte, chose to settle in Holland. The Marquis and his wife prospered in their new homeland, becoming prominent members of Dutch society and influential enough to procure a diplomatic post for one of their sons. In the 1690s, Jean de la Motte, Jacob's grandfather, was appointed the Dutch Consul in Dublin, Ireland.[1]

It was while he was serving in this post that Jean met a young English woman named Sarah Hill, the sister of Charles Hill, an English merchant living and working in Ireland. Apparently, Sarah made a lasting impression on Jean, for soon after meeting her he made some life-changing decisions: he became an English subject, Anglicized his name to John Abraham Motte, and asked her to marry him.[2] The wedding took place sometime before 1700, as their first child was born on November 29th of that year — a little boy named Jacob.[3] He was followed by two girls: Sarah Katherine and Anna.

John, anxious to establish himself in one of the English colonies in the New World, sailed to Antigua in late 1703, leaving his family in Ireland to await the outcome of his mission. While in Antigua, John was fortunate enough to be introduced to John Perry, a wealthy investor who was looking for someone to establish and manage several plantations for him in the colony of Carolina. Finding the prospects in Antigua unpromising, John accepted the position with Perry and sailed to Charleston, arriving there in 1704.[4]

John found Carolina much to his liking, and after establishing plantations in Christ Church Parish for his employer, he set himself up as a merchant in Charleston, specializing in the Indian trade. Charles Hill, John's brother-in-law, also immigrated to Carolina during this time and, like John, established himself as a merchant and Indian trader.[5] In 1707, John was named Commissioner of the Indian Trade — a position he held for the rest of his life.

Having established himself respectfully, John felt it was time to reunite with his family and in 1709, he brought his wife and children to Charleston. Sadly, two years later, in August of 1711, John Abraham Motte died, leaving his widow with three young children to raise.[6] Fortunately for Sarah, her brother was well-established in the colony and was able to help her settle her husband's estate and provide for the education of her son Jacob. It was undoubtedly through Charles Hill's efforts that Jacob acquired an apprenticeship with the merchant Francis LeBrasseur.

On October 22, 1713, just one month before his thirteenth birthday, Jacob Motte Sr. began his training with LeBrasseur. Seven years later, when he had completed his apprenticeship, he was offered a partnership in his uncle's business.[7] As a junior partner in the firm of Charles Hill and Company, Jacob was now in a position to think about marriage and starting a family. In 1724 he married Elizabeth Martin, the daughter of Patrick and Hannah Martin. The couple would eventually have nineteen children together — of which three sons and seven daughters lived to adulthood. Jacob Motte Jr., the oldest of their three surviving sons, was born on October 15, 1729.

Jacob, like Rebecca, was born into a world of wealth and privilege. In 1725 Jacob's father left his uncle's company and opened his own business. In 1731 he expanded his business by building a large wharf on property bequeathed to him by Robert Tradd on the east side of Bay Street. With the completion of Motte's Wharf, his business prospered, and during the next twenty years, Jacob Motte Sr. became one of the three largest merchant-bankers in Charleston.

Jacob's father was also active in government. He was chosen as a vestryman for St. Philip's Parish, and then elected to represent that parish in the General Assembly from 1739 to 1743. He was also active in promoting the welfare of the city, being a member of both the Charleston Library Society and the South Carolina Society — a charitable organization dedicated to promoting education. He was also a benefactor of the school for Indians and enslaved Africans established in Charleston by the Society for the Propagation of the Gospel in Foreign Parts, a social and benevolent organization devoted to education. In 1735 he joined with other wealthy merchants and lawyers in Charleston to form and finance the first fire insurance company in America — the Friendly Society for the Mutual Insuring of Houses Against Fire.[8]

Unfortunately, on November 18, 1740, a devastating fire swept through Charleston, destroying over 300 buildings, many of which had been insured by the Friendly Society. The financial loss to the owners of the insurance company was great and, as a consequence, the Friendly Society went out of business. To make matters worse, among the 300 destroyed buildings were warehouses along the docks containing valuable stores of rice, deerskins, and timber. Therefore, some of the merchants who backed the insurance company not only had the company loss to contend with, but also the loss of revenue from their mercantile businesses. Topping the list of merchants whose businesses suffered the most was Jacob Motte Sr.

However, Jacob was resilient and determined, and went to work to recoup his fortunes. Then in 1743, while he was representing St. Philip's Parish in the legislature, he received an unexpected boon. Gabriel Manigault resigned as the Public Treasurer and recommended him as his successor. The Commons House complied by electing him to the post, and on May 7, 1743, Jacob Motte Sr. resigned his seat in the House and was sworn in as the Public Treasurer.[9]

It is not exactly clear where the Motte family lived while Jacob was growing up. Like other prominent merchants, Jacob Motte Sr. had a place in the country. Known as Mount Pleasant, the Motte country seat was located in Christ Church Parish, and it is possible the family lived there for most of Jacob's childhood. At some point Jacob Motte Sr. moved his family into a large brick house at 69 Church Street — a rental property that he occupied for many years. The house was conveniently located near Jacob's office and store on Motte's Wharf. It was also close to the house where Robert Brewton and his family lived.[10]

In 1745, when his father died, Robert Brewton inherited the bulk of his father's estate, including a townhouse on the southwest corner of Tradd and Church Streets — a few houses up from the house he owned at 71 Church Street. In 1745 Robert sold that house to his brother-in-law Jordan Roche and moved his family into the house that had belonged to his father.[11] The Brewton family were near neighbors to the Motte family — a very convenient arrangement as the Powder Receiver and the Public Treasurer needed to work closely together.

When his father became the Public Treasurer, Jacob was fourteen years old and likely had already begun an apprenticeship with a merchant in town. It appears that all three of the Motte sons eventually went into some kind of commercial business, but as the oldest son, Jacob was the one most likely destined to follow in his father's footsteps and become a merchant-banker. Therefore, it would have been appropriate for him to enter into an apprenticeship when he was twelve or thirteen years of age.

As close neighbors, the Brewton and Motte families would have exchanged social visits and Robert and Jacob Sr. would have conferred together frequently on public business. And with two households full of children, it is likely that the Motte and Brewton children played together or even attended the same dancing class. However, while it is tempting to picture Rebecca and Jacob practicing the steps of the minuet together or rolling hoops in the yard, it must be remembered that Jacob was eight years older than Rebecca. When the Brewton family moved back to Charleston in 1745, Jacob was sixteen years old and working hard at his apprenticeship, hardly noticing the young Brewton girls — all under the age of twelve — living up the street from him.

In October of 1750 Jacob celebrated his 21st birthday. He had likely finished his apprenticeship by this time, and was in partnership with either his father or another merchant in town. It was common practice for an established merchant to offer a partnership to a young man just entering trade — the young man generally being a relative or close family connection. It was an excellent way for newcomers to gain experience and acquire the capital needed to open their own businesses while minimizing their risks. Jacob Motte Sr. had gotten his start in trade by becoming a partner in his uncle's company, and it would have been natural for him to either take his son into partnership, or to arrange a partnership for him with another merchant.

Commerce is always a risky business, and this was especially true in the 18th century when wars, the weather, fire, accidents, and even political issues could hinder commerce — causing financial loss, or even complete ruin for merchants. In September of 1752 it was the weather that dealt the merchants, along with the rest of Charleston, a stunning blow. The town was struck by a hurricane of such magnitude that it was thought to be the most severe storm ever to hit the city. It damaged houses and businesses alike. Among the many places destroyed by the storm was Motte's Wharf, with its warehouses full of rice and naval stores. It was a two-fold disaster for Jacob Motte Sr.

When he became Public Treasurer in 1743, Jacob had been struggling to recuperate financially from the great fire of 1740. Thinking that an infusion of money might help accelerate his recovery, he began to make loans to himself from the public treasury. With the money he borrowed, he was able to start new ventures, and his business began to prosper. In fact, he was doing so well that he was in the process of paying back the loans when the hurricane struck.

Unfortunately, the destruction caused by the storm made it impossible for Jacob to continue the payments. As a result, he was compelled to send a written memorial or statement to the Commons House of Assembly explaining that he had been "impoverished by his losses in the hurricane" and needed more time to repay what he owed to the public treasury.[12] In the 18th century using public money or public office for personal gain was not illegal or even considered unethical — it was merely one of the perks of being a public official. However, if money had been borrowed, it was imperative that it be repaid.

Jacob Motte Jr. was probably not connected with his father's business at this time, but he would, understandably, have been concerned about his father's affairs — especially when he discovered that the committee appointed to examine his father's books was having difficulty deciphering his accounts. It appears that Jacob Motte Sr. kept very poor records and the committee had to struggle to obtain an accurate picture of his financial standing.

Nevertheless, they were finally able to determine that he owed the public treasury £90,000 in South Carolina currency. At this point Jacob Motte Sr. declared bankruptcy. He was allowed to keep his post as Public Treasurer, but was forced to place his entire estate — plantations, commercial property, and enslaved workers, plus "his plate, chinaware and household furniture" into the hands of a board of trustees appointed by the Council and Commons House of Assembly.[13]

In spite of his financial difficulties, Jacob Motte Sr. continued to be well liked and respected by his peers and there appears to have been no stigma attached to the Motte name. Therefore, when Jacob Motte Jr. appeared in society, he would still have been considered a very eligible bachelor. It was probably during this time, as he made the rounds of various social events, that Jacob began to notice Rebecca Brewton among the groups of young ladies present.

Jacob and Rebecca were probably already acquainted, but they would not have known each other very well. However, there were ample opportunities to further their acquaintance in the future, for they would attend many of the same parties, balls, musical evenings, and other social events that made up the "season" in Charleston. Since he was only in his early twenties at this time, Jacob was probably in no hurry to form a lasting attachment, content just to enjoy socializing with his peers — male and female.

In the spring of 1754, while Jacob and Rebecca were in the process of becoming better acquainted, trouble was brewing in the remote western regions of Pennsylvania and Virginia; the French and Indian War was about to begin. Although most of the fighting would take place in the northern colonies and Canada, the progress of the war would have been of great interest to the Motte and Brewton families. In 1755 the British formed a special regiment to counter the unconventional military tactics used by the French and their Native American allies. Known as the 60th Royal American Regiment of Foot, its members were recruited from both the North American colonies and Europe.

Isaac Motte, Jacob's younger brother, and Thomas Pinckney, the son of William and Ruth Brewton Pinckney and, therefore, Rebecca's cousin, were both officers in the 60th Regiment.

Two years later, the war in North America became part of a larger global conflict. In 1756 the Seven Years War broke out in Europe, pitting Great Britain and Prussia against France and Austria. The fighting in this war was not confined to the continent of Europe but took place wherever European countries had colonies or trading stations: India, the Far East, and the West Indies. This global war was of great concern to South Carolina's merchants and planters, having a major impact on the trans-Atlantic and West Indian trade.

In February of 1757, in the midst of anxiety over the war which the British appeared to be losing, the Motte family suffered a great personal loss: Elizabeth Martin Motte, Jacob's mother, died. She and Jacob's father had been married for thirty-three years. After mourning his mother's death, Jacob apparently turned his thoughts toward his future and began to seriously contemplate marriage and starting a family. In 1758, at the age of twenty-eight, he felt that he had found the woman he wanted to spend the rest of his life with — twenty-year-old Rebecca Brewton. His feelings were reciprocated, and the two were married on June 11, 1758, four days before Rebecca's twenty-first birthday.

It would have been viewed as an excellent match. The Brewtons and Mottes were both large, well-connected families with backgrounds in commerce and finance, and the young couple was now linked, by blood and marriage, to many of the most prominent families in colonial South Carolina.

The Motte fortunes took another turn upward the next year, for on April 7, 1759, the Commons House of Assembly dissolved the trust and conveyed Jacob Motte Sr.'s property back to him. He had repaid all the money he had borrowed.[14]

Chapter Three
Rebecca and Jacob

Rebecca and Jacob began their married life together in Charleston in the summer of 1758. Although they had a house in town, the couple would have also wanted to have a place in the country — not just a country seat, but a plantation that would supplement Jacob's mercantile business by providing him with his own supply of rice to market abroad. Therefore, when Thomas Lynch, Jacob's brother-in-law, offered to sell him Fairfield, one of his plantations in Santee — the region around the North and South Santee Rivers — Jacob eagerly accepted the offer.

The Motte's new plantation was located in a prime rice-producing area on the South Santee River, about forty-five miles north of Charleston. There was an owner's house already on the property. Built by Thomas Lynch's father around 1730, the house stood on a bluff overlooking the river, surrounded by a grove of live oaks. It had four rooms on the first floor, and two on the second. Thinking they would need more space in the future as their family increased, Jacob and Rebecca decided to enlarge the house by adding two more rooms to the upstairs portion. The work was completed in 1766.[1]

By the spring of 1759 the young couple had exciting news to relate to their respective families — Rebecca was expecting a child in October. Sadly, Robert Brewton did not live to see his newest grandchild. He died on August 17 at the age of sixty-two. His death meant that the position of Powder Receiver for the province was vacant, and Governor Lyttleton appointed Jacob Motte Jr. to succeed him. It was Jacob's first public office.

It is likely that Rebecca and Jacob did not occupy their house at Fairfield until the addition was complete and were living in

American Patriot and Successful Rice Planter

Charleston in the fall of 1759 when their first child, a little boy named Jacob, was born. Childbirth was a risky procedure in the 18th century, both for the mother and the baby — indeed, fifteen percent of infants born in South Carolina died before their first birthday.[2]

The Mottes baptized their son on the 25th of October and, sadly, buried him three days later.[3]

While Rebecca and Jacob were dealing with the loss of their son, they, along with the rest of Charleston, were unaware of an enemy lurking in the far western regions of the colony — silent, invisible, and deadly. It was small pox. The disease had been raging unchecked through the Native American populations in the frontier areas of South Carolina and Georgia for several months, and in December, soldiers returning from an expedition against the Cherokee brought the disease to Charleston. By January the city was engulfed in a wholesale smallpox epidemic. Many people fled the city, businesses were closed, and hundreds sought inoculation. By April, it has been estimated, over three-quarters of the 8,000 inhabitants of Charleston had been infected with smallpox either naturally or by inoculation, and one person in every eleven had died from it.[4]

Rebecca and Jacob seem not to have been affected by the epidemic. Either they had previously had smallpox and were immune, or they were two of the many inhabitants who went through the inoculation process. Although inoculation for smallpox had been practiced for centuries in Asia and Africa, in Europe and the Americas it was a controversial procedure. It involved deliberately injecting fluid from a healing smallpox lesion into the body of a healthy person, giving that person a mild form of the disease and, most importantly, an immunity from future attacks.

However, there was a risk involved, as it was not unheard of for people to catch a virulent form of the disease from the inoculation and die from it. Anne Loughton Smith, Rebecca's half-sister, and her family were all inoculated. Sadly, Anne was one of the few who did not survive the procedure. She died in February of 1760 at the age of 38.[5]

In 1740 Anne had married Benjamin Smith, a wealthy merchant and the owner of a large plantation in Goose Creek Parish. He was also a prominent member of the Commons House of Assembly, serving on several important committees and as Speaker of the House from 1755-1763. Anne also left four children: Tom aged twenty, Anne who was fifteen, Susannah aged six, and a little boy named William who was two years old.[6]

It was a devastating blow for the Smith and Brewton families. Anxious to assist in any way they could, Rebecca and Jacob offered to take the six-year-old Susannah into their home and raise her as their own. It is likely that Anne also came to live with them at that time, and that William, too, stayed with them for a while — at least until his father remarried eight months later. At the age of two, William would have little recollection of his mother, and no time to form an attachment to his Aunt Rebecca. It would have been a simple matter for Benjamin and his new wife to take the little boy into their household to raise.

With the girls, however, it would have been different. They would have felt the loss of their mother more deeply and, being well-acquainted with their Aunt Rebecca, would have felt quite comfortable with her. The best thing Benjamin Smith could do for his daughters, then, would be to leave them in Rebecca's care.

With the addition of Anne and Susannah to their household, Rebecca and Jacob's family had suddenly doubled in size. It was to grow even more. In the early fall of 1763, Rebecca and Jacob found themselves the proud parents of three healthy baby girls: Mary, born in September 1761, Elizabeth (Betsey), born in August 1762, and Frances (Fanny), born in September 1763. In addition to producing three children in three years,

Rebecca also had domestic and social obligations to fulfill, along with attending to the needs of her nieces. It was an incredibly busy, but happy, three years.

While Rebecca was occupied with childbearing, motherhood, and domestic affairs, Jacob was taking his place in the political world. In May of 1760, the Commons House appointed James Reid to be the Powder Receiver, leaving Jacob free to run for a seat in the legislature.[7] Since representatives were not required to live or own property in the parish they represented, Jacob was able to run for his first elected office in the newly created parish of St. Mark's. He won that election, and went on to represent the parish again in 1761. The next year Jacob ran in a special election to represent St. Helena's Parish in the Port Royal Sound area. However, he returned to represent St. Mark's Parish in 1764. In Charleston, Jacob was a member of the South Carolina Society, the Charleston Library Society, and the Fellowship Society.

In the early part of 1763, the world had cause for celebration: on February 10th the Treaty of Paris was signed, ending the long and bloody war that had been raging for nine years in North America, and seven years in the rest of the world. The end of the war meant that the seas were once again safe for commerce — a great boon to both planters and merchants. It also meant that Lieutenant Isaac Motte and Lieutenant Thomas Pinckney could return home after several years of hard campaigning in Canada and the West Indies.

Rebecca and Jacob would have given Jacob's younger brother a warm welcome when he returned home, inviting him to dine with them regularly or join them in the evenings for informal gatherings. Rebecca's well-known skills as a hostess would have been reason enough for Isaac to accept these invitations, but apparently he discovered an even greater attraction at the Motte house than his sister-in-law's hospitality — eighteen-year-old Anne Smith, Rebecca's niece. As the attraction between the two increased, Rebecca and Jacob could not have helped being pleased — it was in all respects, an excellent match. Anne Smith and Isaac Motte were married in December of 1763.

In the meantime, the end of the war, which had been hailed with great joy in the thirteen colonies, was being viewed with mixed feelings in England. On the one hand, the British were happy — they had just won a great victory. Under the terms of the Treaty of Paris, Great Britain had gained Canada from the French and Florida from the Spanish, leaving them in control of all of North America east of the Mississippi River. On the other hand, while it was a notable victory, it had also been an expensive one — the national debt now stood at £148,000,000.[8] Regrettably, there would be more expenses in the future, as it would be necessary for the British to keep ten thousand troops stationed in North America not only to defend against possible Native American attacks on the frontier, but also to enforce the Proclamation Line of 1763 which prohibited settlement west of the Appalachains.

Should not the American colonists help defray some of the costs? Certainly, they had benefitted from the outcome of the war and would also benefit from having soldiers stationed on the frontier. Determined to raise revenue from the American colonies, the British Parliament began the passage of a number of acts that would eventually drive loyal British subjects like the Brewtons and Mottes into rebellion.

The first of these acts was the Sugar Act, passed in 1764. Designed to curtail smuggling, the act was aimed primarily at the New England colonies where smuggling was widespread and, therefore, raised few eyebrows in South Carolina, where there was little illicit trade. Rebecca, busy with her little girls and niece, and Jacob, concerned with his mercantile business and the rice production at Fairfield, most likely did not give the Sugar Act a second thought. It would be the next act, the Currency Act, prohibiting colonial governments from issuing paper currency, that would cause them to sit up and take notice.

The colonies did not have their own money, and British coins were not readily available; therefore, many of the gold and silver coins in circulation were the foreign coins obtained in trade with the West Indies. Regrettably, most of the foreign coins did not stay in South Carolina, but were sent to England to pay for the goods imported by the colonists. From time-to-time colonial legislatures issued paper currency to pay for public works or, in time of war, for supplies for the militia — they had done so during the French and Indian War.

The currency was paid out to workers or suppliers who were then supposed to use it to pay their taxes, at which time the government would retire the bills. However, the bills often changed hands several times before being turned back in, and sometimes the currency stayed in circulation long after its expiration date. It was not a perfect system, but paper currency made it possible for the average person to quickly and easily pay for goods and services.

Therefore, when the Currency Act was passed, the people of South Carolina were stunned. To make matters worse, the act also prohibited the continued use of any expired bills. The removal of large amounts of paper currency from circulation had a devastating effect on an economy already suffering from a post-war slump. Trade between the colonies and with foreign and British merchants was seriously hampered — a great concern to Jacob and his associates.

Then in 1765, hard on the heels of the Currency Act, Parliament passed the Stamp Act. The act required that all printed materials — legal documents, licenses, newspapers, playing cards, etc. — contain an embossed revenue stamp indicating that the tax on it had been paid. This was the first time a non-maritime tax had been imposed on the colonies by the British Parliament. Already irritated by the passage of the Sugar and Currency Acts, people in all the North American colonies rose up in angry opposition, maintaining that the British constitution protected its subjects from taxation without their consent.

Opposition to the Stamp Act was so great that stamp tax agents either resigned or agreed to suspend their work until Parliament had time to review the situation. With no one to stamp the paper, the courts could not function, licenses could not be issued, and shipping ground to a halt. The port of Charleston was essentially closed for thirteen weeks and, by the first of February, approximately 1,400 ships were lying at anchor in Charleston harbor.[9] Merchants in London, missing the revenue they were accustomed to receiving from the colonies, put pressure on the crown and Parliament, and the British government backed down. In March of 1766, King George III signed the repeal of the Stamp Act.

By this time, the work on the house at Fairfield was complete, and the Motte family took up residence in their country home. At this point Jacob seems to have transferred most of his political activities to his country parish — St. James Santee. In 1767 and 1769, he served as a Justice of the Peace for the parish, and later he would represent St. James Santee in the legislature. In 1768 he undertook to build a new parish church there.

As Lowcountry planters, the Mottes naturally followed the pattern set by other planters: they spent the winter months in the country at Fairfield, and returned to Charleston for the summer. This was done for health reasons. The summer months were considered the "sickly season" in the country, and most rice planters came to Charleston in the late spring or early summer to avoid contracting "country fever" or malaria.

At this time, people did not understand the cause of malaria — a tiny parasite injected into a person by the bite of an infected mosquito. Nor did they know that mosquitoes like to breed in the still, fresh water ponds and swamps found on their Lowcountry plantations. They also did not understand why Charleston, surrounded by salt water and fanned by ocean breezes, thereby attracting fewer mosquitoes, was healthier — they just knew from experience that it was, and so flocked to town.

Following this pattern, Rebecca and Jacob were most likely in town in May of 1766 when the news that the Stamp Act had been repealed reached Charleston. The entire town erupted into a celebration: church bells rang throughout the day, bonfires were lit, and at night there was a grand illumination of the city.[10] No doubt Rebecca and Jacob joined in the celebration with the other townspeople, and like everyone else, they paid scant attention to the second bill signed by the king — the Declaratory Act, which affirmed the right of Parliament to tax the colonies.

Charles Townshend, Chancellor of the Exchequer, then introduced the Revenue Act, which placed a duty on all tea, glass, lead, paper, and paint imported into the colonies. It was passed by Parliament and signed into law by the king in June of 1767. At the same time, the king signed the American Board of Customs Act, replacing the Board of Commissioners of Customs located in England with a Board of Commissioners situated in Boston, with the thought that a Board of Commissioners located in the colonies would be more effective in collecting taxes there than one located three thousand miles across the ocean.

The Revenue Act and the American Board of Customs Act were part of a series of acts known collectively as the Townshend Acts. While Charleston's artisans and tradesmen were vehemently opposed to the Revenue Act, the merchants in town were more concerned about certain provisions of the American Board of Customs Act. According to the act, commissioners of the customs were to station themselves in every port, and all revenue cases were to be heard in admiralty courts where there was no jury, and the accused was assumed guilty until proven innocent.

In the northern colonies, the reaction to the Townshend Acts was more zealous, and merchants in port towns began to organize and form associations to protest the acts by agreeing not to import non-essential British goods until the repeal of the Townshend Acts. While the port of Boston was ready by October of 1767 to implement a non-importation agreement, there was little interest among the merchants in Charleston to follow suit. They preferred to wait and see.

While the merchants of Charleston were conducting business as usual and waiting to see what effect the American Board of Customs Act might have on their businesses, the Mottes were settling in at Fairfield and getting used to life on a plantation. Although Rebecca and Jacob had owned Fairfield for several years, it is doubtful whether they had actually lived there for any length of time, and so residing in the country would have been a new experience for them. However, Rebecca was determined, resourceful, and, most likely, had no difficulty adjusting. With three daughters under the age of six and a nine-year-old niece in the house, she probably never experienced a dull moment.

Sadly, on December 16, 1767, this happy scenario was shattered — the oldest Motte daughter, six-year-old Mary, died, plunging the household into deep mourning. However, just as she had done in the past after the death of a loved one, Rebecca grieved for her daughter and then moved forward with her life. She was soon pregnant again, and gave birth the next year to another little girl. It was not unusual for parents during this time period to give the name of a deceased child to a new baby — consequently, the Mottes decided to remember their first daughter by naming their new daughter Mary.[11]

In early 1768 Rebecca's life in the country was rendered more pleasant by the acquisition of a new neighbor who would prove to be an invaluable friend. In February of that year Daniel Horry, a widower and the Motte's neighbor at nearby Hampton plantation, remarried and brought his new wife, Harriott Pinckney Horry, back to Hampton to live. Harriott was the only daughter of Charles and Eliza Lucas Pinckney and, although only nineteen years old, had considerable experience in plantation management, having helped her widowed mother manage the several large plantations that had been part of her father's estate.

Here, then, was an intelligent and knowledgeable young woman with whom Rebecca could exchange ideas and discuss the business of plantation life. Harriott, in turn, would have found in the slightly older woman a friend whose advice and support she could rely on. With only three miles separating Fairfield from Hampton, the two women had no difficulty in visiting each other regularly. Rebecca was pregnant and already the mother of two little girls when Harriott first came to live at Hampton in February of 1768. How comforting it must have been for Harriott to have Rebecca close by when, in a few months, she found that she was also expecting a child.

Harriott clearly valued Rebecca as a close friend and neighbor. Thomas Pinckney was Harriott's younger brother and one of her favorite correspondents. In answering a letter from her, in which she had obviously lamented the fact that Rebecca was returning to Charleston, he wrote: "I am sorry to hear Mrs. Motte is coming to town, but rejoice that you will have some consolation for her loss in Mrs. T. Lynch."[12] Rebecca and Harriott would remain close friends for the rest of their lives.

Back in Charleston, support for a non-importation association was growing as more and more merchants were becoming upset by the actions of the customs officials and admiralty judges appointed by the king. These officials were, for the most part, not native South Carolinians, but Englishmen — placemen — who had been granted their government posts as a reward for their political loyalty and whose primary concern was personal financial gain. The American Board of Customs Act gave them an opportunity to enrich themselves at the expense of the merchants and planters of South Carolina.

Under the new act, ship owners whose vessels had been wrongly seized could not sue a customs official for damages if the judge ruled that the official had probable cause for the seizure. This meant that the owner had to pay the court costs and had no recourse to recover his expenses in a court of common law. Unfortunately, it did not matter if the ship owner proved to be innocent, the judge almost always ruled that the customs official had probable cause.

The ship owner, the defendant, would then be sentenced to pay the costs of the suit — anywhere from £100 to £150. The fact that admiralty judges were entitled to a percentage of the fees they imposed on defendants made the matter even more repugnant. Rather than lose time and money, many vessel owners found it more expedient to offer the customs official an incentive — a bribe — not to seize their vessels.[13]

It is not known whether Jacob was ever hauled into court by customs officials or had to pay a bribe, but even if he had not been a victim of the American Board of Customs Act, he and other merchant/planters would have realized that they were all potential victims. Therefore, in July of 1769, when an agreement not to import non-essential British goods was drawn up, Jacob and other Charleston merchants lined-up to sign the document.

It was not only the men in South Carolina who resented the actions of the British government. Rebecca and other women in the colony would have been just as incensed as their male

American Patriot and Successful Rice Planter

counterparts over the behavior of customs officials and the acts of Parliament — they just had no way to express their views except in the privacy of their homes or in letters to friends and family. Then the non-importation agreement was implemented and women finally had a way to express their opinions in public: they could show their opposition to the Townshend Acts by refusing to buy non-essential British goods.

Women in all thirteen colonies enthusiastically supported the boycott on British goods. It became fashionable for women to serve a hot beverage brewed from herbs in their parlors after dinner instead of the usual tea and to appear in public in gowns made of homespun rather than the beautiful silks and fine linens imported from England. The *Virginia Gazette* of December 1769 reported that, on the thirteenth of the month, a ball had been given by the Virginia legislature "for the entertainment of Lord Botetourt," the Royal Governor. At the ball, a spirit of patriotism "was most agreeably manifested in the dress of the Ladies... who, to the number of near one hundred, appeared in homespun gowns."[14] It is hard to imagine that Rebecca and other women in South Carolina did not also appear in public wearing homespun.

In the end, thanks in great part to the cooperation of the women in the colonies, the non-importation strategy proved successful. Colonial trade was cut in half, and British merchants were unhappy. As a result, in the spring of 1770, Parliament repealed the Townshend duties on glass, lead, paper, and paint but kept the duty on tea to remind the colonies that it had the right to tax them. The repeal had the desired effect as most colonies, satisfied with the partial victory over Parliament, began to relax restrictions on the importation of British goods. However, in order to send a message to the British government, the boycott on tea did not cease.

South Carolina was an exception. The colony had wanted Parliament to repeal not only the Townshend Duties, but also all the offensive measures that had been adopted since 1763.

Hoping to wring more concessions from Parliament, South Carolinians had continued the embargo longer than the other colonies. However, by December of 1770, the boycott was proving too difficult to maintain, and the colony's leaders voted to end it, while keeping the embargo on tea in place. As a result, nothing changed in the American Board of Customs Act, and customs officials and admiralty judges continued their abusive policies while merchants and planters continued to be annoyed by their behavior.[15]

In June of 1770 the Motte family was saddened by the death of Jacob Motte Sr. He passed away on June 17 at the age of sixty-nine. It was customary in the upper levels of society at that time for family members to clothe themselves in black for the funeral of a loved one and to send black gloves or scarves to those people who were expected to attend the funeral. The deceased's house, coffin, and the carriage carrying the coffin would be draped in yards of black crepe, the horses decked out with black feathers. However, Article III of the non-importation agreement emphatically stated: "we will give no mourning, or gloves or scarves at funerals."[16] All use of black cloth, which was imported from England, was to be avoided. Therefore, it seems safe to assume that Jacob's father was laid to rest without the usual black accoutrements.

Jacob, as the oldest son, would have inherited much of his father's business interests and, as one of the executors of his last will and testament, had not only his father's personal estate to settle, but also his accounts as Treasurer. It is likely that Jacob was heavily involved in settling his father's affairs for the next three years and therefore, did not serve in the government. Jacob would not hold political office again until 1774. By that time, the relationship between the colonies and the mother country had deteriorated to the point that the colonies were planning to hold a general congress in the fall to consider a united response to the actions of the British government.

Chapter Four
The Road to Revolution

From 1771 to 1773, while Jacob was busy settling his father's estate, the situation between the colonies and the mother country remained unchanged — tea continued to be taxed, and the colonists continued to refuse to buy it. Then in 1773, a new crisis emerged as Parliament tried once again to assert its right to tax the colonies and, once again, tea was at the center of the controversy.

The colonial boycott on tea had had a devastating effect on the East India Company, the prime supplier of British tea, and the company was now on the brink of bankruptcy. In May of 1773, Parliament came to the company's rescue by passing the Tea Act which granted the East India company a monopoly on the sale of tea to the North American colonies.

In the fall of 1773 colonial leaders in Charleston learned that the East India Company was planning to send simultaneous shipments of tea to the four major ports in North America: Boston, New York, Philadelphia, and Charleston. They also learned that leaders in the north were planning to refuse to accept the tea as a protest against Parliament's right to tax them. South Carolina's leaders decided to follow their example. Therefore, in early December, when a ship arrived in Charleston harbor carrying two hundred fifty-seven chests of tea, the merchants to whom the tea had been consigned refused to receive it. People from all over the colony were then asked to sign a pledge promising "not to import or buy any tea taxed for raising a revenue in America."[1]

In Boston the response to the arrival of the tea was not so mild. Under the leadership of Samuel Adams, members of a group known as the Sons of Liberty loosely disguised as Mohawk Indians boarded ships anchored in Boston harbor and threw £10,000 worth of the East India Company's tea into the water. In Charleston the reaction was one of shock. The destruction of private property was not something most South Carolinians could condone, and if the British response to the incident had been more moderate, there would have been little sympathy in South Carolina for Samuel Adams and the Boston Sons of Liberty.

However, the British response was vindictive and harsh, designed to intimidate the rest of the colonies by making an example of the Massachusetts colony. In March, Parliament passed the first of a series of acts later referred to as the Intolerable Acts. The acts proposed to close the port of Boston to all commercial traffic, move the trials of royal officials and soldiers who committed capital crimes to a more favorable location, and revoke the charter of the Massachusetts colony and alter its form of government.

The news of the passage of these acts caused outrage and indignation in South Carolina. Undoubtedly, the "Intolerable Acts" formed the main topic of conversation in the Motte's drawing room, as it did in drawing rooms all across Charleston. If the British government could behave in such a manner to one colony, it could behave in the same manner to any or all of the remaining colonies. Therefore, when the Massachusetts legislature called for representatives from all the colonies to meet in Philadelphia the following September, South Carolinians were ready to comply.

It was on a hot, sticky day in July 1774 that delegates from all parts of South Carolina crowded into the Great Hall of the Royal Exchange and Customs House to choose men to represent the colony in Philadelphia. Having selected Henry Middleton, John and Edward Rutledge, Christopher Gadsden, and Thomas Lynch as representatives, the delegates then took up another important matter — coordination of colonial protests against

British policies. A committee, consisting of fifteen merchants, fifteen tradesmen, and sixty-nine planters, was appointed to monitor events and oversee all planned protests. Known as the Committee of Ninety-nine, it would serve for a time as the de facto government of South Carolina. In 1774 Jacob Motte was ready to resume his place in public service once again. He was appointed to the Committee of Ninety-nine and also served that year as a justice of the peace for the city of Charleston.

Delegates from all the colonies except Georgia convened in Philadelphia for the meeting of the First Continental Congress in September of 1774. Since the non-importation agreement of 1769 had resulted in the repeal of most of the Townshend duties, the delegates were willing to try economic pressure once again to bring about the repeal of the Intolerable Acts. They voted to establish a Continental Association that would not only prohibit the importation of British goods, but also the exportation of colonial goods to Great Britain, Ireland, and the West Indies.

Since the non-exportation part of the proposal put forth by the Continental Congress would have serious consequences for South Carolina planters, the Committee of Ninety-nine called for elections to be held in all parts of the colony for representatives to meet in Charleston to discuss the issue. The First Provincial Congress met in Charleston in January of 1775 and, after much debate, voted to join the Association. Non-importation was to start immediately, while the non-exportation phase was to begin in September of 1775 if the Intolerable Acts had not been repealed by that time.

January of 1775 found the Mottes at Fairfield. Jacob was not a member of the First Provincial Congress, therefore, there was no need for him to be in town. Jacob and Rebecca had planned to return to Charleston in February but were forced to delay their departure until later in March. Rebecca and her niece Susannah were both in ill health.[2] Whether the two women suffered from the same disorder or different ones is not known, but

Rebecca was reported to be in a great deal of pain. However, family and friends were happy to hear that by March 9, both she and Susannah were improving.[3]

Upon returning to Charleston, Rebecca and Jacob would have found people there quietly optimistic about the repeal of the Intolerable Acts. It was thought that the sugar planters in the West Indies, who depended on the North American colonies for their food and other necessities, would put pressure on the British government to revoke the acts. Rumors to that effect abounded in town. Rebecca and Jacob, along with the rest of their fellow South Carolinians, would have held their breath and waited for confirmation of their hopes.

However, as the short days of winter slowly lengthened and spring burst forth in the gardens of Charleston, alarming news reached the colony. On April 19 the British packet ship *Swallow* arrived in Charleston carrying a small mail pouch containing letters and documents for royal officials. The pouch, intercepted by political leaders in Charleston, contained a very revealing letter outlining the intention of the British government to use force to compel the colonies into submission. The next day the Provincial Congress appointed a secret committee to take charge of the arming and defense of South Carolina.

It was just two weeks later that a schooner arrived in Charleston harbor from Salem, Massachusetts, bringing news of the fighting at Lexington and Concord. The Provincial Congress, called into an emergency session, met on June 1 and voted to raise two infantry regiments and one regiment of mounted rangers. Officers to lead the regiments were then voted on, with Christopher Gadsden and William Moultrie elected as colonels of the First and Second Regiments. Isaac Motte, one of the most experienced military men in the colony, was elected lieutenant colonel of the Second Regiment, while Charles, the youngest Motte brother, was selected as one of its captains.

In June of 1775, while South Carolinians were busy arming themselves, Lord William Campbell was on his way to Charleston to take up his position as the new royal Governor. He came to his new post with the unenviable task of reigning in the protests against British policies. To his dismay, upon his arrival, he found that the colony had established an extra-legal legislature — the Provincial Congress — that operated independently of British control and influence. The colony had also raised an army. When a delegation from the Provincial Congress delivered an address to him explaining why they had done these things, he responded by refusing to recognize the Provincial Congress.[4] It did not bode well for the future.

In spite of not being recognized by the governor, elections were held on August 7 and 8 for the Second Provincial Congress. Jacob Motte was elected as a delegate from St. James Santee, while Rebecca's brother Miles Brewton was elected as one of the delegates from Charleston. Once the elections were over, Miles would have felt at liberty to pursue a plan he most likely had had in mind for some time — a trip to the northern colonies. In July of 1774 Miles had written to Josiah Quincy, an acquaintance in Boston: "I will strain a point to pass the next summer among the Northern Colonies. It is a country I long to see."[5] Miles, who had entertained Quincy on several occasions during his visit to Charleston in 1773, promised to visit him in Boston.

In January, Miles put a notice in the *South Carolina Gazette:* "… I intend to leave the Province early in the Spring… and may be absent for a considerable time…" He then asked all who owed him money to remit their payments as soon as possible.[6] However, events taking place in the Massachusetts colony in the spring of 1775 made a visit there impractical. Also, Miles was a member of the First Provincial Congress and there were issues that the congress needed to address in the spring and early summer. Consequently, Miles postponed his trip.

However, once the elections for the Second Provincial Congress were over, he would have felt comfortable in leaving the colony for a few months — the congress was not due to meet until December. On August 24, then, Miles and his wife and children set sail for Philadelphia. Following the well-established tradition of women being useful to their male relatives, Rebecca and Frances would have promised their brother they would look after his house at 27 King Street during his absence.

When Miles Brewton set sail for Philadelphia that August, it was the Patriots, those who supported colonial protests against British policies, who held the upper hand in South Carolina. Royal government was at a standstill, and the colony was, in effect, being governed by the extra-legal Provincial Congress. It was not all smooth sailing for the Patriots, however, for there were a number of Loyalists, or Tories, in the colony who supported the king and his ministers.

The Motte family was firmly on the side of the Patriots. Rebecca's husband and brother were in the Provincial Congress — a sure sign of Patriot leaning as no Loyalist was likely to serve in an extra-legal legislative body that was not recognized by the royal governor. Two of her brothers-in-law were in the military, which was also not likely to have Tories in its ranks. The sole reason for the formation of an army was to confront the British should they attack South Carolina as they had the Massachusetts colony, and no self-respecting Loyalist would ever volunteer to take up arms against the king.

Rebecca was not shy about showing her support for the Patriot cause, either. Elizabeth Trapier, a young lady from the Georgetown area and a staunch Patriot, was Harriott Horry's cousin by marriage and one of her favorite correspondents. In August of 1775 Elizabeth wrote to Harriott expressing her annoyance with people who did not support colonial protests against the British, especially those who had come to South Carolina and made their fortunes and "now spurn at their benefactors, & betray the place that has been their Asylum." As a postscript to her letter, she added: "I honour Mrs. Mottes Patriotism."[7] Rebecca was obviously deeply committed to the Patriot cause from the very beginning. However, what she did to excite Elizabeth Trapier's admiration will probably never be known. We can only wish Elizabeth had been more specific.

During the summer, while keeping up with the political happenings in the colony, Rebecca would have noticed that a certain captain in the 2nd South Carolina Regiment was paying a great deal of attention to her niece Susannah. His name was Barnard Elliott, a thirty-five-year-old widower with extensive lands in St. Bartholomew Parish, Amelia Township and St. Peter's Parish. He had been a member of the Royal Council, but had resigned his seat in May, and in June had been elected to the position of captain in the 2nd South Carolina Regiment. His affections for the twenty-one-year-old Susannah were reciprocated and the couple named January 1 as their wedding date.

Meanwhile, the Continental Congress, in an attempt to bring about a reconciliation between the colonies and the mother country, had drafted a petition to send to the king. Known as the "Olive Branch Petition," it assured the king of their loyalty, their desire for a reconciliation, and an end to the fighting in the north. Unfortunately, the king rejected the Olive Branch Petition unread, and on August 23, proclaimed the colonies to be in a state of rebellion.

Since Charleston was now considered to be in rebellion, the Council of Safety, the group charged with overseeing the defense of the city, thought it prudent for the Patriots to take control of Fort Johnson, an earthwork fort standing on the east end of James Island guarding the entrance to the harbor. It was not only the main naval defensive site for the city of Charleston, but it was also the repository of most of the round shot for the city's heavy cannon. It was essential, the council thought, for the Patriots to keep the fort and its armaments intact. Consequently, Colonel Moultrie of the 2nd South Carolina Regiment was ordered to take the fort before the British could disarm it. Colonel Moultrie gave the command to Lt. Colonel Isaac Motte, who saw the mission through.

While Colonel Motte's men were busy taking control of Fort Johnson, the royal governor had dissolved the Commons House of Assembly and sought refuge aboard the British sloop-of-war *Tamar* which was hovering off the coast. Lord William Campbell, the last royal governor of South Carolina, was on board a few days later when a strange flag was hoisted over Fort Johnson. It had a field of blue with a silver crescent in the upper left-hand corner, and had been designed by William Moultrie on the orders of the Council of Safety. Moultrie had modeled the flag on the attire of the soldiers of the 2nd Regiment who wore uniforms of blue with a silver crescent on the front of their caps. It was the first American flag to be displayed in South Carolina.[8]

The *Tamar* was soon joined by the *Cherokee* and the two ships took up position at the entrance to the harbor effectively blockading it, causing a shortage of provisions and supplies in town. Rumors of a possible naval invasion were rampant in the city that fall, and the rumors coupled with the presence of British warships outside the harbor caused many townspeople to flee to the country.

It is not known whether the Mottes joined the exodus from the city or not. However, whether they went to Fairfield or stayed in town, at some point they learned that the ship carrying Miles Brewton and his family was long overdue in Philadelphia, casting a cloud of gloom over the family and friends of the passengers on board. Anxiety over their fate was then added to the fears of an invasion by the British.

When the Second Provincial Congress, of which Miles was a member, met in the late fall, there was still no word on the fate of the ship or the passengers. In the forlorn hope that Miles might yet return to participate in the assembly, the Provincial Congress kept his seat open for him.[9] The uncertainty of whether the family was alive or not must have had a draining effect on Rebecca and Frances. They would have still been conscientiously looking after their brother's house and, on every visit, must have wandered through the rooms wondering if Miles and his family would ever return to live there again.

However, Rebecca had to put that worry aside, as she had other matters that needed her attention in the late fall. She had a wedding to plan and on January 1, 1776, she saw her niece happily married to Barnard Elliott. Just five days later, the British fleet left South Carolina, sailing south down the Georgia coast. Everyone then breathed a great sigh of relief.

In the meantime, the Council of Safety was taking no chances. The British fleet might have left the area, but it could always return, and the members wanted to be ready. Therefore, the council ordered Colonel Moultrie and members of the 2nd Regiment to occupy Sullivan's Island and begin the construction of a fort on the southern shore facing the entrance to the harbor.

The British might have left the Charleston area, but they had not forgotten about the South. In fact, it was quite the opposite, as officials in London were planning a campaign to conquer the southern colonies. They assumed it would be an easy task, as they had been assured by disposed royal governors from the South that the majority of the colonists there were loyal and would rise up to support the king once British troops landed on southern shores. Acting on that assumption, Sir William Howe, commander-in-chief of British forces in North America, ordered Sir Henry Clinton and a small force to sail from Boston at the end of January. Clinton was to rendezvous at Cape Fear in North Carolina with Loyalists in the area and await the arrival of Lord Cornwallis, who was sailing from Ireland with seven regiments. Together they would then launch an attack in the South.

When the Second Provincial Congress met in Charleston in January, it was painfully apparent to all that Miles Brewton, a prominent leader in the colony and one of its wealthiest citizens, had tragically perished at sea with his entire family. Therefore, the congress ordered a special election to be held in February to fill his seat.[10] Of the five children born to Robert and Mary Griffith Brewton, only two now remained — Frances and Rebecca.

The Second Provincial Congress had important work to do. Since the royal governor and other British officials had left with the British fleet at the beginning of January, there was no official government in South Carolina. The congress needed to write a temporary constitution and establish an interim government to ensure that order was preserved in colony until an understanding could be reached with Great Britain. The new constitution basically kept the old form of government in place, with a few minor changes such as replacing the governor and lieutenant governor with a president and vice-president. John Rutledge and Henry Laurens were then chosen to hold those positions.

At the same time, 180 miles north of Charleston at Cape Fear, Sir Henry Clinton was waiting impatiently for Cornwallis's fleet to arrive. It was not until the beginning of May that all the ships in the British fleet had assembled, enabling Clinton to make plans to launch an attack in the South. While he was mulling over whether to attack in the Chesapeake or Charleston, scouts sent out on a reconnaissance mission down the Carolina coast returned to report that the Americans were in the process of building a fort on Sullivan's Island. Only the southern wall, which faced the channel, and the western side were defensible. The walls on the east and north were only seven feet high. Clinton then decided to attack Charleston.

The news of the approach of a fleet of British ships sent women and children scurrying from Charleston to seek refuge

American Patriot and Successful Rice Planter

in the countryside. Since the male members of their families remained in town to defend it against the British attack, the women and children tended to band together in groups at nearby plantations — far enough away to feel safe, but close enough to get the latest news from town. Susannah Elliott left Charleston, but it is not known whether Rebecca and her daughters also left. It is possible they sought refuge at Fairfield.

As the women and children fled, reinforcements poured into town to swell the ranks of the South Carolina regiments and militia units gathered to defend the city — all in all a total of 6,500 men. To direct them, the Continental Congress had sent Major General Charles Lee. Lee was an experienced and able soldier, but an eccentric with a bad temper and a habit of expressing his views with brutal candor. He was not at all impressed with the half-finished fort on Sullivan's Island calling it "a slaughter pen." Nevertheless, he threw his energies into building up the defenses in the town and trying to correct some of the defects of the island fort.

On June 4, the British fleet arrived at the bar guarding the entrance to the harbor. Three days later, the ships began the slow process of crossing the bar to anchor in Five Fathom Hole — a spot just inside the entrance to the harbor, but out of range of the guns at Fort Sullivan. Ten days later, on June 17, the British began landing men on Long Island, located north of Sullivan's Island, and separated from it by a seventy-five-foot wide inlet.

If the British troops crossed the inlet onto Sullivan's Island, they could attack Fort Sullivan from the rear while the warships battered it from the front. To confront the twenty-two hundred British regulars now encamped on Long Island and prevent them from crossing the inlet, the Americans sent Lt. Colonel William Thomson, an experienced Indian fighter, with a force of seven hundred eighty militia and regulars. They threw up earthen breastworks reinforced with palmetto logs and waited for the British to make a move.

The long-awaited British attack took place eleven days later on June 28. At 11:30 in the morning, the defenders at the fort on Sullivan's Island looked up to behold twenty-eight ships in full sail moving through the channel. The fort was defended by members of the 2nd South Carolina Regiment commanded by Colonel Moultrie. His second-in-command was Lt. Colonel Isaac Motte. Captain Charles Motte was also on duty at the fort that day.

The enemy ships formed two lines and a heavy cannonade began between the fort and the ships. Colonel Moultrie had thirty-one guns and a limited amount of gunpowder to use against eight British men-of-war boasting a total of two hundred sixty guns. To conserve powder, Moultrie ordered the cannons to be fired every ten minutes and only when a clear shot presented itself. Fortunately, the fire from the fort was deadly accurate and caused several of the British ships to run aground while others were badly damaged.

After approximately ten hours of bombardment, the fort still stood. It had been built of palmetto logs — a double row of the logs encircled the fort and the space between the exterior and interior walls had been filled with sand and marsh clay. Palmetto wood is soft and does not splinter; therefore, the palmetto log walls of the fort absorbed the cannonballs hurled at them and did not shatter.

On June 29, Major Barnard Elliott wrote to his wife, Susannah. Originally a captain of the 2nd Regiment's company of grenadiers, Barnard had been elected a major in the 4th Regiment of the South Carolina Line — an artillery unit — when it had been created in November of 1775. He was stationed at an artillery battery in town during the battle and he described what he had seen and heard about the battle to Susannah:

> The firing continued till near 10 o'clock, and I have the pleasure to inform you that we have lost but ten men and twenty-two wounded…

My old grenadier, Serj. [sergeant] Jasper, upon the shot carrying away the flag-staff, called out to Col. Moultrie: "Col., don't let us fight without our flag." "What can you do?" replied the Col.; "the staff is broke." "Then, sir," said he, "I'll fix it to a halbert, and place it on the merlon of the bastion, next to the enemy;" which he did, through the thickest fire. General Lee crossed from Haddrell's to Sullivan's in the heat of the cannonade, and was at the fort. His letter to the President says he never saw but one cannonade equal to this, though he has seen many; nor did he ever see officers and men behave better, nor could any in the world exceed them.[11]

Clinton's plan to have his men on Long Island ford the inlet that separated that island from Sullivan's Island and attack the fort from the rear came to nothing. As Major Elliott explained to his wife: "The enemy made three attempts to land on the north of Sullivan's during the cannonade, but were each time repulsed without any loss on our side."[12]

The Americans expected the British to renew their attack the next day, but they did not. Those who had evacuated the town decided to return, secure in the knowledge that, should the attack be renewed, they would have enough warning to be able to evacuate. Susannah Elliott, at the urging of her husband, was back in the city by June 30. She brought with her a project she had started after receiving her husband's letter the day before.

Inspired by her husband's description of the bravery of the men of the 2nd Regiment in defending Fort Sullivan, Susannah wanted to present the regiment with a gift to show her admiration for their valor. Therefore, she had designed a pair of elegantly embroidered silk colors or flags — one of a fine blue silk and the other of red silk. In the center she had embroidered a green wreath with a red bow at the bottom. Inside the wreath was a furled red and blue flag, and embroidered in yellow around the inside of the wreath were the words: "Vita Potier Libertas" — Liberty Rather than Life — with the date 1775 (the year the regiment was created) placed above the red ribbon. In the right-hand corner were the initials of the 2nd Regiment stitched in yellow.[13]

On July 1, Susannah presented the colors to Colonel Moultrie and Lt. Colonel Motte with these words: "Your gallant behavior in defense of liberty and your country, entitles you to the highest honors; accept these two standards, as a reward, justly due to your regiment. I make not the least doubt, under heaven's protection, you will stand by them, as long as they can wave in the air of Liberty." Colonel Moultrie responded with a promise that the banners would be honorably carried and never tarnished by the 2nd Regiment.[14]

Susannah Elliott had been part of the Motte household for fifteen years, from the time of her mother's death in 1760 when she was just six years old until her recent marriage. Rebecca had been like a mother to her. It is not surprising, then, that a young woman raised by Rebecca Motte had conceived such a distinctive and moving way to show her patriotism.

To the relief of all the inhabitants of Charleston, the British did not renew their attack. Instead, sailors spent the days after the battle working to repair the damage inflicted on their ships by the Americans. When that was completed, the British then began the slow process of transferring soldiers to the waiting transports. On July 14, the British ships began to slip away one by one and by August 2, they were completely gone.

The people of Charleston then began to celebrate their victory. In the middle of the festivities, an express arrived with the news that on July 2, the Continental Congress had declared the United Colonies to be free and independent states, and on July 4, a Declaration of Independence, drafted by Thomas Jefferson, had been adopted. On August 5, the city of Charleston celebrated the signing of the Declaration of Independence with a grand parade consisting of the men of the Carolina regiments, their officers, and various civilian dignitaries led by

President John Rutledge. They marched to the Liberty Tree, where the Declaration of Independence was read aloud to the assembled crowd by a jubilant Major Barnard Elliott.[15]

Chapter Five
War Comes to the South

When the euphoria of the victory over the British and the adoption of the Declaration of Independence had subsided, Rebecca and Frances were faced with the melancholy task of settling their brother's estate. In his last will and testament, Miles stipulated that if his sons died without issue, his estate was to be "equally shared and divided" among his two sisters, Frances and Rebecca, as "tenants in common."

Among the property to be divided between Rebecca and Frances was Miles Brewton's beautiful house on King Street with its handsome drawing room, a hall that stretched across the front of the second floor of the house. Josiah Quincy, a visitor from Boston who dined there on his visit to Charleston, was so impressed with the room that he recorded in his diary: "The Grandest hall I ever beheld, Azure Bleu sateen-window Curtains, rich bleu paper with gilt, Mashee Borders most elegant pictures, excessive grand and costly looking glasses, etc."[1]

The outside of the house was equally impressive. The two-story brick house was built over a high basement and stood on a large parcel of land that stretched from King Street westward to Legare Street. There was a paved courtyard in the front of the house which was separated from the street by a "handsome iron fence." Two marble stairways on either end of a large portico rose gracefully to the front entrance. On the west side, or back of the house, a double stairway led to an extensive pleasure garden, and at the far end of the garden, Miles had placed a garden house which contained a stone bathing pool. The property was, to say the least, unique.[2]

At some point, Frances and Rebecca must have decided that one of them should live in the house and maintain it. After all, the house had been important to their brother. He had spent a great deal of time, money, and effort building and furnishing it, and he would have wanted it to remain in the Brewton family. How they decided who should occupy the house is not known, but ultimately it was Rebecca, Jacob, and their three daughters who moved into 27 King Street.

Among the several plantations owned by Miles Brewton, there were two that Rebecca and Frances decided to claim as individual properties — Greenwich and Mount Joseph, both located on the Congaree River in St. Matthew's Parish. On September 9, 1777, Rebecca renounced her half of Greenwich plantation to Frances.[3] In return she received sole ownership of the Mount Joseph plantation consisting of thirteen hundred acres, a stock of cattle, horses, and other farm animals, plus plantation tools and utensils.[4]

While she was busy attending to the details of the inheritance from her brother, Rebecca could not have helped to recognize certain signs — bouts of nausea in the morning and an overall feeling of lethargy — indicating that she was pregnant. Having turned forty in June and not having had a child for nine years, the news must have come as something of a shock to her. She may have also felt a little anxious. In the 18th century, the risk of death in childbirth increased with the number of pregnancies and with age as older women faced extra dangers when giving birth. Happily, Rebecca's sixth child, a little girl, was born without any difficulty in December of 1777 or early January of 1778. Her baptism on January 9 at St. Philip's Church in Charleston suggests that she was born at the Miles Brewton House, probably in the withdrawing room located on the second floor next to the large drawing room, which tradition indicates was used as a birthing room for generations of Brewton women. She was named Rebecca Brewton Motte after her mother, but the family always called her Becky.

In March of 1778 the Second Provincial Congress met again in Charleston and the first item on its agenda was to replace the temporary constitution, which had been written two years earlier, with a permanent one. The members made only a few changes to the old constitution. They decided to have a governor as head-of-state instead of a president, and to replace the Legislative Council — the upper house of the legislature — with a full senate. The lower house remained the same, with additional seats allocated to the backcountry. Jacob Motte, a member of the Second Provincial Congress, was also a member of the General Assembly under the new constitution and would continue to represent St. James Santee in the lower house until the British captured Charleston in the spring of 1780.

Under the new constitution all male inhabitants over the age of sixteen were required to swear an oath of allegiance to the state of South Carolina, promising to defend it from the armies of the king. Loyalists who were unwilling to take the oath had sixty days in which to leave the state, and many of them did just that, making their way back to England or removing to Canada or the British colonies in the West Indies. Some of the king's supporters, however, went to join the British at St. Augustine in Florida. Once there, they formed into militia units under Governor Tonyn and began to conduct raids into western Georgia and South Carolina.

General Howe, Commander of the Continental Army in the South, and the governor of Georgia felt the best way to stop these raids was to eliminate Florida as a base from which to launch them. Therefore, they proposed to invade Florida, capture Fort Tonyn located just over the border, and then march south to attack St. Augustine. Having only a small force of continental soldiers under his command in Savannah, Howe wrote to General Moultrie requesting that one of the South Carolina regiments join the expedition. Consequently, on April 19, the 1st South Carolina Regiment marched out of Charleston for Savannah.

Rebecca and her daughters would have followed the progress of the Florida expedition very carefully, as there was one officer in the 1st South Carolina Regiment whose welfare was of particular importance to them — Major Thomas Pinckney, Harriott Horry's younger brother. In an age where there were only limited means of obtaining news, letters were a valuable source of information and were more often than not shared with family and friends. Thomas wrote frequently to his sister, telling her how the campaign was progressing and making light of the hardships facing the army. Harriott would have, quite naturally, shared his letters with others — most especially the Motte family.

Harriott would have had a very special reason for wanting to share Tom's letters with the Mottes — she was anxious to promote her brother's long-standing attachment to Betsey, Rebecca, and Jacob's oldest daughter. As early as February of 1775, Tom had written to Harriott from Charleston: "I am going…directly to Mr. Lynch's where I shall see the adorable Miss Betsey."[5] The thirteen-year-old Betsey was visiting Tom and Hannah Motte Lynch, her aunt and uncle, in Charleston at the time.

In the 18th century, young unmarried women did not correspond with young men unless they were engaged to or related to them. As Tom could not exchange letters with Betsey, he relied on his sister to convey his feelings to his "charmer," as he often referred to Betsey. In one letter he wrote: "If chance should throw my charmer in your way I charge you to make strong love for me."[6]

Just as Harriott shared Tom's letters with the Motte family, she also shared any news or information she had about Betsey with her brother. In June of 1778, while on the campaign in Florida, Tom wrote to his sister:

"…your writing particularly of the Person whose allurements you think so powerful with me, renders your Correspondence to be sure still more agreeable, as I find my Inclination increases, … and I am now in East Florida a more fervent Admirer than I was three Months ago in Charles Town."[7]

Harriott most likely shared that little bit of information only with Betsey.

The Florida campaign cannot be said to have been a great success, as it was hampered by heat, humidity, mosquitoes, and the inability of the army to deliver supplies in a timely manner — all of which took its toll on the soldiers. Fortunately, when the Americans reached Fort Tonyn, they found that the British had abandoned and burned it. The leaders of the expedition then wisely decided that, since they had accomplished one of their objectives, they could in good conscience return home. Consequently, at the end of July, the remnants of the 1st South Carolina Regiment, gaunt and tired, marched into Charleston and received a warm welcome. No doubt, Rebecca and her daughters were part of the crowd that welcomed the regiment home.

Besides welcoming the soldiers of the 1st Regiment, there was another reason for Charlestonians to celebrate that summer. In May, the Continental Congress had ratified a treaty of alliance with France. The impressive American victory at Saratoga in the fall of 1777 had proved to the French that the Americans were capable of facing the British on the field of battle. As a result, France declared war on Great Britain and signed a treaty of alliance and trade with the United States. The entrance of the French into the war in America was hailed with great joy by the Patriots.

The British, however, found the French declaration of war very disturbing. The French were a traditional enemy located just across the English Channel, and they posed a serious threat. While there was no fear that the Americans would invade the homeland, attack the valuable sugar islands in the West Indies, or threaten British possessions in India, Africa, and the Mediterranean, there was a very good chance that the French would do so. The War for America had suddenly been transformed into a global conflict with more at stake than the possibility of losing thirteen colonies.

The British were in a quandary. They had a tough decision to make. What was more important to them: the thirteen North American colonies, or their possessions in the rest of the world? The southern colonies with their rich crops of indigo, rice, and tobacco were worth defending, they decided, but the northern colonies were a different matter — they were expendable. The war in the North was bogged down and at an impasse — it was time to move the military action to the South.

British officials in London built their strategy for the southern campaign on the assumption that most of the people in the South were loyal to the king. In fact, loyalist support was fundamental to the success of the southern strategy. The plan was to "roll up the South" by first conquering Georgia, re-establishing it as a royal colony, and turning it over to loyalist forces to govern and control. The same procedure would then be followed in the Carolinas and Virginia. American Loyalists, along with token British troops, would then hold the South for Great Britain, freeing up soldiers to fight in other parts of the world.

With the plan in place, the British set about to implement it. On November 27, 1778, a force of thirty-five hundred British soldiers set sail from New York for the city of Savannah. At the same time, Major General Augustine Prévost and his troops began marching north from St. Augustine. Upon receiving word of Prévost's advance towards Georgia, General Howe quickly sent off an express to General Moultrie in Charleston, requesting that he send the South Carolina regiments to his aid as quickly as possible.

Unfortunately, by the time General Benjamin Lincoln, who was replacing Howe, and his men arrived, the British were in control of Savannah and what was left of Howe's army was encamped on the South Carolina side of the Savannah River. All General Lincoln could do was to join forces with the remnants of Howe's command, and establish an encampment in Purrysburg, a little town on the South Carolina border.

Within ten days of taking Savannah, the British had all of coastal Georgia under their control. They then marched north up the Savannah River and occupied Augusta, and by the end of the month, were in command of the outlying areas of the state. General Lincoln did not have a force strong enough to oust the British from Augusta. All he could do was to take up a position in the surrounding countryside to try to disrupt the flow of supplies to the British from the backcountry. Georgia was, for all practical purposes, a royal colony once again, and it would remain so until 1782.

Having secured Georgia, the British were anxious to move on to South Carolina. On April 30, General Prévost, with two thousand men, crossed the Savannah River. As Prévost and his men pushed north, they burned and plundered plantations in their path, carrying off able-bodied slaves to be sold later in the West Indies. The people of South Carolina were thus introduced to the realities of war with all its brutality and wanton destruction — something they had not experienced before. It was an ominous portent of what was to come.

Prévost continued his drive all the way to Charleston Neck and was within one mile of town by the middle of May when he received word that General Lincoln was making all possible speed to Charleston. Not wanting to be caught between the defenders in town and Lincoln's approaching army, Prévost decided to withdraw, leaving a contingent of men on Port Royal Island near the town of Beaufort, approximately seventy miles south of Charleston. The rest of the British army returned to Savannah.

American Patriot and Successful Rice Planter

June found Major Thomas Pinckney and the 1st South Carolina Regiment in the Port Royal area keeping an eye on the British forces on the island in case they decided to use the area to launch a new campaign against Charleston. However, by the middle of July, it appeared the British were content just to hold Port Royal Island for the time being. Since the General Assembly was meeting in Charleston, General Lincoln requested that all officers who were members of the legislature return to the city. Major Thomas Pinckney was a member of the legislature, and so returned to town.

Once in Charleston, Tom had a more important matter on his mind than attending to his legislative duties. His affection for Betsey Motte had not abated, and now that the war had come to the South, he did not know what the future might bring. He had no idea when he would be able to get leave to visit Charleston again, and he wanted very much to make Betsey his wife. He decided to take advantage of this opportunity and ask for her hand in marriage.

His proposal could not have come as a complete surprise to Rebecca and Jacob. They must have been well-aware of Tom's longstanding regard for their oldest daughter. It must have given Rebecca a great deal of pleasure to know that her daughter was to marry the brother of her closest friend — it would make the ties between the two families even stronger. Rebecca and Jacob approved the match, and the couple was married on July 22, 1779. Betsey was one month short of her seventeenth birthday, and Tom was twenty-eight.

The Carolina countryside was quiet during the remainder of the summer — the inhabitants and soldiers, both British and American, being content to relax and conserve their energy during the long, hot days of August. Consequently, the lull in fighting gave Betsey and Tom a chance to settle in to married life with few distractions. Though the British might be miles away from Charleston on Port Royal Island or back in Georgia for the moment, Betsey, Tom, and everyone else knew that as soon as the excessive heat of summer was over, they would return to try to take the capital.

Of course, the best way to avoid another British attack on Charleston would be to drive the British out of Savannah. Unfortunately, General Lincoln did not have an army strong enough to achieve this goal. Another plan would have to be devised. After much deliberation it was decided to enlist the aid of the French fleet under the command of Comte d'Estaing, which was now operating in the West Indies. It was suggested to the Comte that he and his fleet take a short respite from cruising in the Caribbean during the dangerous hurricane season and join with American forces in a cooperative effort to re-take Savannah. The Comte agreed to the proposal.

The French fleet arrived off the Georgia coast on September 11 and began to disembark soldiers fifteen miles south of Savannah. By the 16th of the month, three thousand French troops were encamped in front of the British-held city. General Lincoln arrived the next day, September 17, with fifteen hundred men, and on September 23, the French and Americans began to set up camp about one mile from the enemy lines.

Twelve days had now elapsed since the French had landed on the Georgia coast, and the British had used the time to build up their defenses — which were formidable. The only way to take the town would be by siege — a slow but effective method of taking a heavily fortified position. Savannah was completely surrounded. The French fleet was blockading the harbor, preventing access to the town by water, while the allied troops were guarding the land approaches.

The French and Americans began to dig their siege trenches at the end of September. But by October 8, the officers of the

French fleet had become impatient and began to urge d'Estaing to lift the siege. The French had only expected to spend a short amount of time on this expedition, and they had already been in Georgia over a month. The hurricane season was coming to an end and d'Estaing's officers were anxious to return to the West Indies. D'Estaing decided to lift the siege and informed General Lincoln "that he must withdraw his force but to prove his desire to serve the cause he offered to cooperate in an assault on the British lines."[8]

General Lincoln had no choice but to agree to what he must have considered an ill-advised attack. The British position consisted of a series of redoubts — small earthen forts mounted with artillery — swinging in a great arc from the swamp below town to Yamacraw Creek on its upper boundary. In front of the redoubts were deep ditches protected by a strong abatis — a barrier made of felled trees with sharpened ends facing outward toward the attacking force. A frontal attack on such a heavily fortified position would be difficult at best.

The main thrust of the allied attack was the Spring Hill redoubt, located on the extreme right of the British defensive works. Colonel Laurens and his Light Infantry, along with the 2nd South Carolina Regiment led by Colonel Francis Marion and members of the Charleston Militia, were the attacking force, and they fought with great determination. The attackers made it through the abatis into the ditch in front of the redoubt where, according to Thomas Pinckney's account of the battle, the two color-bearers "planted their colors on the berm."[9] — the colors referred to were the two flags presented to the 2nd Regiment by Susannah Elliott.

The walls of the ditch were high, and though the Americans made a valiant effort to climb them, they were stopped by heavy, determined fire from the British defenders. The first wave of attackers fell back into the ditch in front of the redoubt, and were replaced by another wave, then another, and another. Soon the ditch was choked with the bodies of the wounded, the dead, and the dying. During the attack, the blue flag also fell into the ditch and one of the color-bearers, mortally wounded, fell upon it in an effort to protect it. It was later found by British soldiers who took it back to England as a trophy of war. When the time came to retreat, Sergeant Jasper, who had so gallantly hoisted the fallen flag during the Battle of Sullivan's Island, grabbed the red flag and managed to bring it back to the American camp, even though he was severely wounded. He died the next day of his wounds.[10]

The Second Battle of Savannah was one of the bloodiest battles of the American Revolution, and the 2nd South Carolina Regiment, fighting once again with valor and distinction, was one of the units that suffered the most casualties. Many of its soldiers fell trying to scale the walls of the ditch in front of the Spring Hill redoubt, while others fell on the field without making it to the abatis. One of those who fell early in the battle was Major Charles Motte, killed while urging the 2nd Regiment forward. His death must have brought great sadness and a deep sense of loss to the Motte family. It was a grim reminder of the personal cost of war.

The French gathered up their wounded, boarded their ships, and sailed away to the West Indies. The South Carolina regiments and militia made ready to return to Charleston, saddened by the loss of so many of their comrades, and greatly disappointed by their failure to take Savannah from the enemy. There was nothing left for them to do but return home and wait for the British to make the next move.

It did not take the British long. Once General Sir Henry Clinton, the British commander-in-chief in North America, learned that Comte d'Estaing and the French fleet had left Savannah, he immediately began to prepare for the second stage of the British plan to "roll up the South." On October 25, 1779, he ordered three thousand soldiers to sail from Newport, Rhode Island to Savannah. Then two months later, on December 26, he followed them, sailing from his headquarters in New York at the head of a sizable force: 8,700 British troops and a fleet of 50 ships.

The British fleet made its way south in January of 1780 and landed in Savannah at the end of the month. After a short interval ashore to recover from the voyage, men, horses, and equipment were re-loaded aboard the ships and the fleet sailed northward, landing at Simmons Island (now called Seabrook), just thirty miles south of Charleston on February 11. Once the slow process of landing men, horses, artillery, and supplies had been accomplished, Clinton began to move his army slowly and methodically — first to James Island, and then to the mainland. Clinton had failed in his first attempt to take Charleston in '76 because he had made mistakes. He was taking no chances on this occasion, as he was not about to fail a second time.

By early March, the British army had crossed over to the mainland and had begun establishing encampments on the banks of the Ashley River. From his headquarters, Clinton could now look out over the river to view his objective: the city of Charleston — the jewel of the South — sparkling in the sun. The British then began to build batteries on the banks of the Ashley River. The Siege of Charleston was about to begin.

Chapter Six
British Occupation of South Carolina — Part One

When the British army appeared on the south bank of the Ashley River in early March and began to build batteries and establish encampments, many people in Charleston thought it prudent to make arrangements to leave the city as quickly as possible. Once again, plantations in the countryside were called on to serve as places of refuge for women and children, and Fairfield was no exception. When the Motte family evacuated Charleston, they took with them an expanded household, as Rebecca invited some of their female relations and their children to join them.

The entourage that gathered at Fairfield that spring included: Rebecca, Jacob, their three daughters, Fanny, Mary, and Becky; Betsey Pinckney, who was expecting her first child in the summer; Martha Motte Dart, Jacob's sister, and her children, and Mary Brewton, Rebecca's niece by marriage. Mary, or Polly as she was called, was the widow of John Brewton, the son of Rebecca's half-brother Robert — the sibling who had gone to live in Bermuda. John had come to Charleston as an adult, and gone into partnership for a time with his Uncle Miles, and when he died of an undisclosed illness in May of 1777, Rebecca had taken the young widow under her wing.[1]

It is not known exactly when the Mottes left Charleston, but they were at Fairfield before April 12, according to a letter from Thomas Pinckney to his sister at Hampton. Harriott had taken refuge there in early March with her children, her mother, Sally Middleton Pinckney, her sister-in-law, and her two daughters. After concluding his letter, Tom added a postscript: "By an Accident for which I cannot account, the

American Patriot and Successful Rice Planter

enclosed [letters] for Mr. Motte and Mrs. Neyle never came to my Hands 'till this Morning. Please to inform them of this Circumstance."[2]

Mr. and Mrs. Neyle were neighbors of the Horrys and Mottes in Santee, and it is apparent from Tom's postscript that both the Neyles and the Mottes had left Charleston by this time and taken refuge in the country. In those days, there was no regular mail service, and the only way to send letters to friends and family in other areas was to entrust them to an obliging neighbor who was traveling to that region or sending an enslaved servant there on an errand. It would have been common knowledge in town that Tom, who was stationed on Sullivan's Island, was corresponding regularly with his wife at Fairfield, and his sister at Hampton. Therefore, anyone in Charleston who had a letter to send to Santee would have sent it to Thomas so he could send it on with his own correspondence.

Meanwhile, the situation in Charleston was rapidly deteriorating — the city was now surrounded on three sides: Charleston Neck, the Ashley River, and the harbor. The only way open was across the Cooper River, and that route was in danger of being closed as the British were hauling boats across Charleston Neck to the river in preparation for landing troops on the other side. Once there they could challenge the Americans for control of the river crossings, eventually sealing off the city and trapping the defenders inside.

It was at this point that General Lincoln suggested that Governor Rutledge and three of his council members should leave town. If Charleston fell, it was important that the government be able to continue functioning in another part of the state. Consequently, on April 11, Governor Rutledge, accompanied by Charles Pinckney II, Daniel Huger, and John Lewis Gervais, left Charleston for Georgetown.

On April 13, the British captured the Patriot supply depot at Monck's Corner — a crossroad near the west branch of the Cooper River thirty-two miles north of Charleston. Three weeks later, they gained control of Lenud's Ferry, a crossing point on the Santee River, and the noose around Charleston tightened. In the town itself, the British bombardment was causing considerable damage, and the number of people killed and wounded was increasing. Provisions were low and people were living on rice, sugar, and coffee — meat was almost impossible to be had.

At the end of April, in desperation, General Lincoln sent Thomas Pinckney to deliver a verbal message to Governor Rutledge, who was in Georgetown trying to rally a relief force, urging him to send whatever troops he had available as quickly as possible. Tom arrived safely and delivered the message, but, unfortunately, before the relief forces had reached the Santee River, they received word that Charleston had surrendered. Tom, bitterly disappointed and with a heavy heart, then headed for Fairfield.

On May 12, at 11:00 in the morning, the South Carolina Regiments of the Continental Line marched out of Charleston to the designated place where they were to lay down their arms. They then marched back to their barracks where they were to remain as prisoners of war until exchanged. Members of the militia were allowed to return home as prisoners on parole — prisoners who had given their word not to take up arms again. All civil officers and citizens in town were also considered to be prisoners on parole. General Clinton, riding into the conquered city, then chose the most beautiful and prestigious house in Charleston as his headquarters: he took up residence in the Miles Brewton House.

The fall of Charleston stunned Patriots throughout the state. Upon hearing the news, militia units in the backcountry quickly disbanded, the men returning to their homes, determined to keep a low profile while the cavalry units that had been operating in the Santee area scattered, seeking a safe haven from the British forces that would inevitably be moving north from Charleston. The Continental army in the South was practically non-existent. Brigadier General Isaac Huger was the highest-ranking Continental officer left who was not a prisoner of war, and Colonel Buford's corps of 350 soldiers newly arrived from Virginia was all that remained of the army.

From his home, where he was recuperating from an illness, General Huger ordered Buford and his troops to withdraw to Hillsborough, the Patriot capital of North Carolina. Governor Rutledge and two of his council members who were also heading for Hillsborough decided to travel along with them. Also joining them was General Caswell and his North Carolina militia, who, like Buford corps, had arrived too late to assist in the defense of Charleston.

General Clinton had every reason to be satisfied with what he had accomplished. He had captured Charleston, and the inhabitants were lining up to swear allegiance to the king just as he had thought they would. However, his mission was not complete; there was still work to be done. The rest of the state needed to be brought under British control, the people in the outlying areas had to be pacified, and a Loyalist militia had to be organized to govern and hold the state for the crown. It was a large undertaking and Clinton wanted to strike quickly while the people of South Carolina were still reeling from the loss of Charleston.

The first order of business was to eliminate what was left of the Continental army in the South. Therefore, a few days after the surrender, Clinton ordered Lord Cornwallis to cross the Santee River and strike at Buford's corps. By May 18, Cornwallis and his army had reached the south bank of the Santee and, while preparing to transport 2,500 men and five heavy artillery pieces across the river, Cornwallis sent one of his regiments, the British Legion, on a special mission.

The British Legion was a regiment of cavalry and foot soldiers made up of American Loyalists recruited from the northern states. The foot soldiers of the Legion were mounted, traveling on horseback to the site of the battle, then dismounting to fight on foot. Lieutenant Colonel Banastre Tarleton, the commander of the Legion, was an aggressive young British officer known for his daring and perseverance. Cornwallis ordered Tarleton and the Legion to go to Georgetown and "chase away or take prisoner all violent enemies to the British Government and to receive the allegiance of the well affected."[3]

When Tarleton and the British Legion reached Georgetown, they were no doubt met by jubilant Tories, who lost no time identifying all the "violent enemies to the British Government" who lived in the Santee area. High on the list would have been Jacob Motte, member of the General Assembly, Major Thomas Pinckney of the Continental army, and Colonel Daniel Horry, commander of the South Carolina Light Dragoons.

Tarleton's favorite method of attack was to catch his opponents off-guard as he and the Legion had done at Monck's Corner, where they attacked the cavalry unit guarding the supply depot at three o'clock in the morning. What better way to capture unsuspecting Patriots than to raid their plantations in the dead of night? It appears that British troops did just that, at both Fairfield and Hampton, appearing at night after everyone had gone to bed, hoping to catch Jacob Motte, Daniel Horry, and Thomas Pinckney unaware. They were only partially successful — they captured Jacob and Daniel, but Tom managed to escape.

There is little documentation for the events that took place at Fairfield during the period between May 18, when Tarleton and the British Legion arrived in Georgetown, and the first part of June, when Rebecca and the women and children gathered at

Fairfield had safely removed to the Motte plantation at Mount Joseph. We can, however, construct a reasonable scenario based on what we know of British policies at the time, information found in the Pinckney letters, and family tradition — anecdotes handed down in the Motte and Pinckney families.

The first written account of Rebecca's experiences during the war came in 1849 when Elizabeth Ellet published the first of her three-volume series entitled *The Women of the American Revolution*. The second volume has a chapter devoted to Rebecca Motte and provides some information about the period just after the fall of Charleston. Ellet wrote:

> Surprised by the British at one of her country residences on the Santee, her son-in-law, General Pinckney [Tom was a general in the War of 1812], who happened to be with her at the time, barely escaped capture by taking refuge in the swamps. It was to avoid such annoyances that she removed to "Buckhead," [Mount Joseph] afterwards called Fort Motte...[4]

This incident could only have taken place in May of 1780.

More light is shed on this event by Harriott Horry Ravenel, who was the great-great-granddaughter of both Eliza Lucas Pinckney and Rebecca Motte. In 1896 she published a biography of her great-great-grandmother entitled: *Eliza Pinckney*, in which she used information gathered from written sources and family tradition. And family tradition, she explained in the preface to her biography, meant: "the stories and accounts of Mrs. Pinckney's grandchildren; the old people to whose conversation I listened in childhood."[5]

One of the stories handed down in the Pinckney family was an account of a night visit to Hampton by the British "soon after the fall of Charles Town." It was reported to be the earliest memory of Eliza Pinckney's four-year-old granddaughter, Harriott Pinckney — the daughter of Charles Cotesworth Pinckney and Sally Middleton Pinckney. According to little Harriott, that night there were many people in the house — her uncles Colonel Horry and Major Pinckney, her Aunt Betsey Pinckney, and others. She was sleeping on a cot at the foot of her grandmother Pinckney's bed when the British came. Major Pinckney made his escape, but Colonel Horry was seized and made to take parole. She also recalled that the soldiers plundered the house, but did not burn it or any of the outbuildings.[6]

It is reasonable to assume that there were two raids that night — one at Hampton and one at Fairfield. The recollections of the four-year-old Harriott, who must have been terrified with British soldiers swarming through the house, would have been vague at best. It is highly likely that the details of the raid at Fairfield became blended into the story of the raid at Hampton as the anecdote was told and re-told over the years and the two raids were condensed into one — becoming part of the Pinckney family lore.

While we do know that Thomas Pinckney managed to escape into the swamp, we do not know exactly what happened to Jacob Motte and Daniel Horry. Presumably they were seized by the British, and it is possible that they were taken away that night and ultimately ended up in Georgetown as prisoners. Daniel Horry had commanded state troops, and so was not a Continental soldier, and may have fallen into the same category as the militia captured at Charleston — a prisoner-on-parole. It is possible that he gave his word not to take up arms again, and was allowed to return home. Under the terms of the surrender of Charleston, Jacob as a civilian may also have been considered a prisoner-on-parole. However, Jacob had been a member of the rebel government and the British may have taken a different view of his status.

As the British occupied areas of South Carolina after the fall of Charleston, they made a practice of rounding up prominent Patriot leaders and removing them to other locations. It was vital to the British southern strategy to have Loyalist militia hold the state for the crown, freeing British soldiers to fight in other places. British officials felt that defiant Patriot leaders set an example for others, and were a deterrent both to the creation of a Loyalist militia and the establishment of a Loyalist government. The solution was to relocate Patriots to other areas of the state.

Tarleton's orders had been to "chase away or take prisoner" those who were not sympathetic to the British cause. Did Tarleton decide to "chase" the Mottes away from the Santee area as well as keep Jacob Motte temporarily in custody? Did he make their relocation a prerequisite for Jacob's eventual release? This is a distinct possibility because some time during the last weeks of May, Rebecca and the extended family that had gathered at Fairfield moved to Mount Joseph. Jacob did not go with them.[7] Presumably he was still being detained by the British.

There had to be a compelling reason for the move. It was between eighty and ninety miles from the Fairfield plantation in Santee to the Mount Joseph plantation in the Congarees. It would have been a long and arduous journey for five women, one of whom was seven months pregnant, and at least six children, ranging in age from three to twelve — not to mention a number of enslaved servants. Rebecca took as many of her belongings as possible — china, cooking utensils, clothing, household linens, wine, foodstuffs, and so forth. She also volunteered to take horses belonging to the Horrys with her to keep them out of the hands of the British.[8] This was not a journey to be taken lightly.

After successfully completing their mission in Georgetown, Tarleton and the British Legion caught up with Cornwallis's army at Nelson's Ferry on the Santee River on May 22. Thanks to information given him by local Tories, Cornwallis had gained some vital news about Buford's forces. They had passed Nelson's Ferry ten days ago, he was told, and even more interesting was the fact that Governor Rutledge and two of his council members were said to be traveling with him.

Cornwallis now saw an opportunity to capture the remainder of the Continental army and the rebel governor of South Carolina in one stroke. However, there was a problem: Buford and his companions had a ten-day lead, and Cornwallis knew he could not overtake them with his infantry. His only chance to catch the Americans was to send the hard-riding British Legion after them. Always ready for a challenge, Tarleton left Nelson's Ferry on the 27th of May with 270 men.

Meanwhile, Buford, happily unaware that he was being pursued, was making his way to Camden where his corps and General Caswell's men were parting company — the general and his troops heading home to North Carolina. Eleven miles north of Camden was Rugeley's Mill, the home of Colonel Henry Rugeley. Despite being a prominent Tory, Rugeley offered Governor Rutledge and his party food and lodging for the night. Buford and his men continued on, headed for an area a few miles south of the North Carolina border called Waxhaws, where they intended to rest.

Riding hard in horrendous heat, Tarleton and his men reached Camden on the evening of the 28th and rested briefly. By two o'clock in the morning, they were ready to leave, and by dawn were at Rugeley's Mill. By a stroke of luck, Henry Rugeley had received word that the British were coming and had managed to hustle these visitors out of his house just before midnight. At Rugeley's Mill, Tarleton discovered that Buford was only twenty miles ahead. Sensing victory, Tarleton continued his relentless pursuit, coming up with Buford's force by three o'clock in the afternoon.

Immediately, Tarleton attacked with his cavalry. The men of the British Legion were known to be utterly fearless and ruthless in battle and also to be reluctant to cease fighting once the attack was over. At Monck's Corner, a French officer fighting with the Americans asked for quarter — offered to surrender — and instead was fatally hacked and slashed by Tarleton's men.

The attack at Waxhaws was even worse as Legion soldiers were accused of hacking down Continental soldiers trying to surrender and cruelly stabbing some of the wounded as they lay on the ground. After fifteen minutes, the battle was over, and one hundred thirteen Americans lay dead on the field, and two hundred three had been captured — one hundred fifty of whom were so badly wounded they could not be transported with the rest of the prisoners.

Whether the accusations of unwarranted brutality were justified or not, Waxhaws was a bloody affair and the ruthless reputation of Banastre Tarleton and the British Legion that had begun at Monck's Corner grew out of all proportion. Tarleton earned for himself the nickname "Bloody Ban" and "Ban the Butcher," and in subsequent battles the words "Tarleton's Quarter" or Buford's Quarter," signifying that no mercy would be given, became a rallying cry for the Patriots.

Having successfully eliminated what was left of the Continental army in South Carolina, Tarleton and his men joined Cornwallis, who had gained control of Camden, a busy settlement one hundred twenty-four miles northwest of Charleston. The town was strategically located on the Great Wagon Road which led north all the way to Pennsylvania. From there the British could control the area to the east and stop any Continental army from invading the state from the north.

In the meantime, Rebecca and her party had reached Mount Joseph after a long and difficult journey. It is not clear from Miles Brewton's will what structures were standing on the Mount Joseph plantation when it came into Rebecca's possession. Since there is mention of cattle and other stock, as well as tools and utensils, it is safe to assume there were outbuildings for both the animals and storage for the equipment, as well as quarters for the enslaved workers and a house for the overseer.

However, there was definitely no owner's house on the property. Therefore, when Rebecca and the others arrived at Mount Joseph, they took up residence in a vacant farmhouse located on an adjacent tract of land. At some point, Rebecca had a large two-or-three-story house built on a high bluff overlooking the Congaree River a few hundred yards south of the farmhouse. The house was finished sometime before January 1781.

When she heard about the trials encountered on their trip, Eliza Lucas Pinckney wrote to Betsey: "it gave us great concern to hear of the frights and hardships you underwent in your journey and the continuance of them since you have been up, the disappointment in your boat must have render'd your situation most uncomfortable."[9] Eliza had some cheerful news for the family at Mount Joseph, however, as a postscript to her letter added that since writing the above, "we have had the pleasure of seeing your Papa, who is now with us, and I shall trouble him with delivering this letter."[10] But it was not Jacob Motte who took the letter to the ladies at Mount Joseph; it was Sampson, one of the Motte's enslaved servants. Jacob Motte was sent to James Island with other Patriot leaders in the Santee area who were considered too dangerous to the restoration of a British government to remain.[11]

While Rebecca and the others were preparing for their move to Mount Joseph, Thomas Pinckney, having escaped from Fairfield, and taken refuge in the swamp, now found himself in a dilemma. He was a soldier without an army — the closest Continental army being far away in the north. He was all on his own. However, he did have a few options. He could travel to Hillsborough with Governor Rutledge and await events there, he could remain in hiding in South Carolina, hoping to join the army that must soon be sent to liberate the state, or he could travel north and offer his services to General Washington. Tom decided on the latter course — but first, he wanted to see his brother in Charleston. He contacted British officials and asked permission to visit his brother and then to travel out of the state under a flag of truce. His request was granted.

On June 2, Tom was allowed a 30-minute visit with his brother in the presence of a third party. He told Charles of his plans to leave the state and travel north to join Washington's army. The two brothers were very close and their goodbyes must have been tinged with great sadness. When Tom left Charleston, he had no idea if he would ever see his brother again. However, there was an even sadder leave-taking in store for him. The British had given him permission to visit his wife at Mount Joseph on his way north.

At some point between June 5, when Tom wrote to his mother from Captain Giles's plantation in Santee, and June 11, when he wrote to her from Camden, he visited Mount Joseph. It must have been incredibly sad for the young couple. Given the uncertainties attending childbirth in the 18th century, not to mention the uncertainties of a soldier's life, the two of them could not have helped but feel they might never see each other again. "However," Betsey wrote to Eliza, "I do all in my power to keep my spirits, and hope for The best."[12]

Having occupied Camden, the British soon marched into the backcountry and occupied Ninety Six, a trading post 175 miles west of Charleston, and then the hamlet of Cheraw on the Pee Dee River just south of the North Carolina border. They went on to establish two important outposts north of Camden, at Hanging Rock and nearby Rocky Mount. They soon held key positions in the state stretching in a great semi-circle from Georgetown in the Lowcountry through the backcountry all the way to Augusta just across the Savannah River in Georgia. The Patriots in the backcountry, stunned by the loss of Charleston and the bloody encounter at Waxhaws, had offered no resistance — even the most ardent Patriot had accepted parole.

General Clinton, satisfied that his plans for the conquest of South Carolina were being successfully implemented, began to make arrangements for his departure. He was planning to take part of the army and return to New York, leaving General Lord Cornwallis in command. Before he left, however, he issued a series of proclamations calculated to reinstate the majority of South Carolinians to the status of loyal British subjects.

Clinton's first proclamation, issued on May 22, had promised amnesty and pardon to all who would once again swear allegiance to the king. He issued another proclamation on June 1, promising that all inhabitants who took the oath of allegiance would be "re-instated in the possession of all those rights and immunities which they heretofore enjoyed under a free British government, exempt from taxation, except by their own legislature."[13] Since "taxation without representation" had been the original cause of the dispute between Great Britain and her colonies, many felt they could in good conscience return to British rule.

Unfortunately, Clinton issued another proclamation on June 3 that undermined the good intentions of the previous ones. Under the new proclamation, the terms of surrender, which had allowed prisoners on parole to remain neutral for the duration of the war, were repealed. After June 20, prisoners on parole were to be restored to all the rights, privileges, and duties of British subjects, would be required to take an oath of loyalty to the king, and would be expected to take an active part in the British war effort. Those who did not swear the oath of loyalty would be considered rebels and traitors and be treated accordingly. As a matter of course, their property would be confiscated.

As the long, hot summer dragged on, those with Patriot sympathies struggled with an ever- increasing sense of dread and despondency. At Mount Joseph, Rebecca, Betsey, and the other women tried to keep their spirits up, but it was not an easy task. In addition to their despair over the Patriot cause, there were other more immediate concerns. Sickness and the British army both visited Mount Joseph. On July 17, Betsey wrote to Eliza:

> ...it gave me pleasure to hear That you with Mrs. Horry and all friends at Santee were in health. I wish we could say The same but the fevers have attacked our Children and Negroes early, Three of Aunt Dart's Children & Mary have for this ten days past been very sick with Fevers and we all expect to have it soon...Mamma joines me in affectionate Love to Mrs. Horry; is sorry to inform her That some person has stole one of her Mares altho she did every thing in her power to save Them; The other Three with one Horse she sends down by Sampson; They are in very bad order as The Army has taken all our provisions & it was not in our power to fed Them. she is afraid if she does not send them away the rest may be taken as They are contunually calling to inquire for Horses. Papa has been gone down a Month to day & we have never heard from him but once; he is on James Island but hope he may be able soon to return to his Family.[14]

Meanwhile, General Clinton sailed away to New York on June 5, confident that he was leaving a state firmly under British control and a population primarily restored to allegiance to the king. He could not have been more mistaken. A storm was brewing in the Carolina backcountry — a signal of the beginning of the end for the British in South Carolina.

Chapter Seven
British Occupation of South Carolina — Part Two

On May 28, 1780, Colonel Thomas Sumter, former commander of the 6th South Carolina Regiment, was at home on his plantation when he received a message that a detachment of British soldiers was headed his way. Gathering a few belongings and grabbing his musket, Sumter and his body servant left immediately and made their way north to the American headquarters in Salisbury, North Carolina. Once there, Sumter let it be known that he was proposing to raise a volunteer army and return to South Carolina to fight the British.

It was not long before militiamen from the backcountry, feeling betrayed by the June 3 proclamation, began to trickle into Salisbury to join him. When they had given their word not to take up arms again after the fall of Charleston, the militia had been promised they would be able to remain neutral during the remainder of the war. They had also been promised that as long as they kept their word they would not be molested by British troops. Now they were being told they had to swear allegiance to the king and take up arms against comrades still in the field of battle or be considered traitors and lose their property. Furthermore, Tory militia were now roaming the countryside, rounding up Patriots, burning their homes, slaughtering their livestock, and abusing their families. As a result, paroled militiamen who would have been content to sit out the remainder of the war grabbed their weapons, saddled their horses, and with grim faces rode north to Salisbury.

Loosely organized under Sumter's leadership, these men were known as Sumter's Brigade. On July 12 at Williamson's plantation, the Brigade won a decisive victory over Captain

American Patriot and Successful Rice Planter

Christian Huck of the British Legion who was commanding thirty-five Legion cavalry, twenty mounted infantry of the New York volunteers, and sixty Tory militia. The British losses were high as only twelve Legion dragoons and twelve Tory militia managed to escape — the rest were either killed or taken prisoner. The Americans had one man killed and one wounded.

Patriot spirits rose as news spread throughout the countryside that partisan soldiers had overwhelmingly defeated regular Loyalists forces, including members of the dreaded British Legion. Militiamen in the Santee area, who had been lying low, emerged and began to form partisan units. In August, these units united under the leadership of Colonel Francis Marion, who — by a stroke of good fortune — was home nursing a broken ankle when Charleston fell and thus was free to assume leadership of partisan fighters in the Lowcountry. In January of 1781, Marion's Brigade was formally established.

As these brigades were being formed, good news arrived from the north. The Continental Congress had appointed General Horatio Gates — the victor at Saratoga — as the new Commander of the Southern Department, and he was on his way to Hillsborough to take command of his army. Tom had gotten as far as Hillsborough when he heard the news and decided to wait there to offer his services to the new commander. Gates arrived in Hillsborough on July 25, accepted Tom's offer of service, and asked him to be one of his aides. Two days later, the army marched out, and Tom's spirits were high. He was returning to South Carolina as part of an army, and they were headed to Camden to retake it from the British.

Choosing the most direct route to his objective, General Gates led his army through the central part of North Carolina, and by August 13 the Americans were encamped at Rugeley's Mill just eleven miles from Camden. Although Gates had 3,000 men with him, two-thirds of his force were inexperienced militia, and he was not anxious to engage the British in battle.

Instead, he intended to build defensive works a few miles north of the city and, with the assistance of Sumter's and Marion's Brigades, cut British supply lines forcing the British commander posted to Camden, Francis, Lord Rawdon, to abandon the town. Because he wanted soldiers to begin building the defensive works early the next morning, Gates ordered a night march. On the night of August 15, the American army set out, traveling south on the road to Camden.

Earlier, on August 9, having learned that General Gates was moving towards Camden with an estimated force of 5,000 men, Rawdon had sent an urgent dispatch to Cornwallis in Charleston. Cornwallis immediately left the city with a small escort and, riding hard through the night, reached Camden four days later to take command of the British forces. Upon hearing that the Americans were encamped at Rugeley's Mill, Cornwallis, thinking he would be facing a force twice the size of his own, planned to surprise the enemy by attacking their encampment in the early morning. On the night of August 15, the British set out traveling north from Camden.

At two o'clock in the morning, with only the light of the stars to show the way, the cavalry forming the vanguards of each army literally ran into each other on the Camden Road. Chaos ensued for the next fifteen minutes. Then each side managed to draw back to collect their wounded and regroup. Cornwallis, to his relief, learned from captured American soldiers that the force facing him only numbered 3,000 — many of them inexperienced militia. Unfortunately, General Gates learned from captured British soldiers that 2,200 battle-hardened British regulars led by General Lord Cornwallis — the "fighting general" — were facing him.

The battle began at dawn. After exchanging artillery fire, the British began to advance on the left side of the American line, comprised of inexperienced Virginia militia commanded by General Edward Stevens. When Stevens warned his men that they would have to use their bayonets after firing a few rounds, the militia, many of whom had just received their bayonets the night before and had no experience using them, panicked and fled. The panic became contagious and spread to the North Carolina militia posted to the left of the Virginians.

Thomas Pinckney was about 200 yards behind the front line with General Gates and others when the first wave of fleeing militia came streaming past them. He immediately rode forward to try to rally the next group of bolting men, while Generals Gates, Stevens, and Caswell tried to stop the first group and make them reform. However, no one could stop the onslaught of fleeing men and General Gates and the others decided to retreat. It was while he was covering their retreat that Tom was wounded, his left leg shattered by a musket ball. In great pain, he managed to ride four miles to the rear of the American line, where the non-combatants encamped with the supply wagons and the baggage train. Major Charles McGill lifted him into a wagon.[1]

The battle of Camden was a disaster for the Americans. The exact number of casualties on the American side is not known, but Tarleton estimated that seventy officers and 2,000 soldiers were killed, wounded or taken prisoner.[2] It was reported that the British Legion chased fleeing Americans for twenty-two miles, capturing or killing many of them hours after the battle was over. General Gates, riding a very fast horse, retreated all the way to Hillsborough.

Tom, of course, knew nothing of what was happening after he was placed in the wagon. The pain of his shattered leg was overwhelming and he fainted. He was found lying there, unconscious, after the battle by Captain Charles Barrington McKenzie of the 71st Regiment. Tom and his brother Charles had both gone to school in England, and Captain McKenzie was an old school friend of Tom's from Westminster.

Fortunately, Captain McKenzie recognized Tom and had him taken into town with the British wounded. The next day, when he visited his friend, Captain McKenzie realized he was likely to lose his leg — and possibly his life — if he did not receive immediate medical attention. Before the Second Battle of Savannah, when Captain McKenzie's brother had been captured by the French off the Carolina coast, Tom had seen to it that his old schoolmate had everything he needed. Captain McKenzie wanted to return the favor, and he persuaded Banastre Tarleton to send the British regimental surgeon to look after Tom.

Meanwhile at Mount Joseph, in the midst of sickness and periodic raids by British troops, Rebecca was helping Betsey prepare for the birth of her baby. The child, a little boy, was born sometime before August 20, and to everyone's delight both mother and baby came through the procedure with little difficulty an extraordinary circumstance given the sickness that prevailed on the plantation. Betsey named her son Thomas, after his father.

The news that her husband had been wounded at the Battle of Camden and taken prisoner probably reached Mount Joseph a day or two after the battle ended — around the 17th or 18th of August. Both bones of his lower leg had been broken and splintered — a compound fracture, which meant that part of the bone was protruding through the skin and there was a great risk of infection.[3] Thankfully, the prompt attention of the British surgeons saved Tom's leg; it would not have to be amputated. Still, Tom was in a great deal of pain and was facing a long and tedious recovery.[4]

Unfortunately, John, Tom's body servant, along with his horses and all his baggage, had followed the retreating Americans to Hillsborough, leaving Tom with just the clothes he had on his back. When news reached Mount Joseph that Tom was without his baggage, Rebecca most likely hurried to put togeth-

American Patriot and Successful Rice Planter

er a package of necessities — soap, comb, and other toilet items, candles, blankets, and perhaps a bottle of wine, which, was thought to reduce the chance of infection. She would have had Sampson deliver the package. It would have been a struggle for her to do so, though, because by the end of August, everyone at Mount Joseph was sick — the only exception being the baby.[5] There was, however, a positive note for Rebecca in the middle of all the sickness — at the beginning of September, Jacob Motte was able to join his family.

In the meantime, the British were treating Tom very well, showering him with "every Mark of kindness and Attention,"[6] as he informed General Gates. Banastre Tarleton, not known for his compassionate treatment of his opponents, sent Tom wine and other "delicacies"[7] and even tried to find the horses his men had impressed from Mount Joseph and give them to Tom since his own horses were missing. Tarleton wrote:

> I am really afraid, (the Captivity of Mr. Mottes Horses being of so long standing) I shall not have the wish'd for Success in finding them out — I have desird the Bearer [most likely Sampson] to try to trac them & you may depend upon my Exertion whatever Situation the Horses are in—
>
> If Mr. Mottes Servant cannot find them, for I do not know them & indeed the whole of my Horses are so changed for the worse since I left them in the Summer that I hardly know any in the Corps; I must adopt other means to obtain you Horses —
>
> I hope you feel yourself as wel as can be expected from the Nature of your Wound: I don't mean to be all Profession, but you always will find me happy to contribute to your Ease and Satisfaction as much as lyes within my Power.[8]

The British, of course, would have been delighted to have so notable a person as Thomas Pinckney change sides and become a loyal British subject once again. The favorable treatment meted out to him was, in part, an attempt to persuade him to do just that. However, their efforts would be in vain, for Tom would remain completely committed to the Patriot cause.

Once again, The British descended on Mount Joseph, but this time they did not come in force — they came one or two at a time and, unlike previous visits, these were most welcome. British officers on their way to Charleston often stopped at Mount Joseph to deliver letters from Tom and give the family first-hand accounts of his recovery. Likewise, when the officers reached Charleston, they called at the Horry townhouse, performing the same service for Tom's anxious relatives there. On their return to Camden, they would stop again at Mount Joseph with letters from the family in town for the Mottes. Communicating with people located a hundred miles or so away was difficult in the 18th century, and the Mottes and Pinckneys were appreciative of the service provided by the officers.

At the end of September, the officer who visited Mount Joseph was able to relate some very good news to the family. Tom's doctor had concluded that the bones in his leg were fairly well joined and strong enough for him to travel — as long as he did not travel by land. Tom and all the members of his family had long thought that Camden, crowded with the sick and wounded, and surrounded by malarial marshes and swamps, was not the best place for him to recuperate. So, as soon as the doctors assured him his leg was strong enough for him to make the journey by water to Mount Joseph, Tom applied to Cornwallis for permission to be paroled to the Congarees — the 18th-Century term for the area around the Congaree River Valley. On September 24, he received permission to go to "Mr. Motte's House where you may remain 'till your wound is sufficiently heal'd to enable you to travel, when you will join the rest of the Field Officers on Parole at Orangeburg..."[9]

Because there was a danger that the bones in his leg might suffer some trauma on the voyage, Tom had to travel lying in his bed.[10] Consequently, a periagua — a large dugout canoe made from a cypress tree — was specially modified to accommodate the bed. Jacob Motte and a surgeon who lived in the Congaree

American Patriot and Successful Rice Planter

area came to Camden to accompany Tom on his journey. The group arrived at Mount Joseph by October 13, and Tom was happily united with his wife and child.[11]

While the bones in Tom's leg were fairly well joined, pieces of shattered bone kept working their way through the skin, causing him a great deal of pain. He had become very thin: "my legs are literally no thicker than a stout Man's Wrist," he wrote to his sister.[12] He was hoping that with the change of air at Mount Joseph and an adequate diet of wholesome food, his condition would improve.

When Tom arrived at Mount Joseph, the situation there must have caused him some concern as most of the residents were sick. "The Justest Information I could give you of this Family," he wrote to his nephew, Daniel Horry, "would be to make a military Return of the Sick & wounded; as the House has been really an Hospital for some time past." Fortunately, by the time Tom wrote his letter, most of the "Patients" — including little Thomas — were getting better. "Your Aunt has got rid of her Fever," Tom continued, " tho' she is still so weak that she fainted two Days ago in extracting a small Piece of Bone from the wound in my Leg; as she has been for a For'tnight past my only Surgeon."[13]

Just as the health of the family was improving, tragedy struck. Benjamin Dart, Rebecca's nephew, the son of her sister-in-law Martha Dart, died — not from an illness but, reportedly, from eating too many "ground nuts." Benjamin was most likely sensitive to nuts and suffered a fatal physical reaction by consuming them. Because allergies were completely unheard of in the 18th century, no one would have understood that it was what he ate, not how much he ate that caused his death. Benjamin's relatives simply believed he had died because "he could not command his appetite."[14]

Rebecca and the rest of the family were just recovering from the shock of Benjamin's death when another disaster hit Mount

Joseph: smallpox. The disease, which had been rampaging through the countryside for several months, finally struck the Congaree plantation in November. When smallpox first made its appearance in the summer, Harriott had received written directions from Dr. Garden in Charleston on the proper procedure for performing inoculations and sent a copy to Rebecca. However, the prevalence of sickness at Mount Joseph during the summer and early fall most likely prevented her from following through.

How many people living on the plantation caught the disease is not known. Smallpox is highly contagious, and anyone who had not been inoculated or who had the disease before would have been vulnerable — family members as well as enslaved workers. Rebecca and Jacob were immune, as they had survived the smallpox epidemic in 1760 — and Thomas had been inoculated as a small child in England.[15] Betsey, though, was vulnerable, and she and the baby were both stricken — Betsey so ill that Jacob was convinced that she would not survive. When this report reached Tom's family in Charleston, they were greatly concerned. The only consolation they had was the fact that Jacob had the reputation of being easily alarmed "at every apprehension of Danger to his Children," leading them to hope that Betsey was not in as much danger as her father imagined.[16]

By early December, the crisis was over, and Betsey and the baby were both recovering — along, it is presumed, with all the others who had been stricken with the disease. All was not well with Tom, though, as his condition was not improving; small splinters of bone were still working their way out of the wound on his leg. Harriott and Eliza had been concerned about "the deplorable State, poor Mr. and Mrs. Motte, and all their family are in, from ill health;"[17] and thought everyone would benefit from a change of location. Especially, though, they urged Tom to apply for permission to come to Charleston, where he could be constantly attended to by a doctor.

In early December, Jacob Motte began to prepare for a trip to Charleston. He may have had business of his own to take care of in town, but it appears that one of his objectives was to obtain permission from the British for Tom to leave Mount Joseph and travel by boat to Santee. Around the 6th of December, Jacob bid the family farewell and set out on his journey.[18]

When Rebecca and her entourage of women and children had made their arduous journey to Mount Joseph in June of 1780, people in the state were still reeling from the surrender of Charleston. Patriot morale was at a low point. But through the long, hot months of summer, the Patriot situation had improved — despite the devastating American defeat at Camden and the absence of a Continental Army in South Carolina. Partisan fighters under Francis Marion in the Santee area and Thomas Sumter in the backcountry had filled in for the lack of a regular army, scoring significant victories over the British. The most important had come on October 7 — when 1,100 partisan fighters from western Virginia and North and South Carolina attacked and overwhelmingly defeated Major Ferguson and his thousand Loyalist militia at King's Mountain.

Now it was the turn of the British and their Loyalist allies to be stunned by unexpected defeat. Making the situation worse for them was ongoing harassment of the king's forces by partisan fighters despite efforts made by the British to stop it. Soldiers in British outposts in the backcountry needed to be re-supplied from Charleston, and supply convoys making the long journey from Charleston were prime targets for partisan fighters — well mounted and able to move swiftly and strike unexpectedly. To combat these attacks, the British decided to establish outposts on the Santee-Congaree River roads to guard the supply routes from Charleston to Ninety Six and Camden.

British supply convoys, their wagons heavy with provisions and supplies, began their journey from Charleston to the interior by crossing the Santee River at Nelson's Ferry and then traveling northwest along the Congaree River Road. At McCord's Ferry, near Mount Joseph, some of the convoys crossed the Congaree and headed to the outpost at Camden, while others continued on to Friday's Ferry, crossed the Saluda River, and headed northwest to Ninety Six.

In the early summer of 1780, the British established an outpost at Nelson's Ferry to protect the crossing there and later that summer appropriated the home of James Cayce, upriver from Mount Joseph, and fortified it. Renamed Fort Granby, it protected the landing at Friday's Ferry for convoys headed to Ninety Six. It now appeared that more outposts needed to be added.

In late summer or early fall, the British fortified Belleville plantation located about a mile south of Mount Joseph. In late December or early January, they built Fort Watson downstream from Belleville on a high abandoned Indian mound overlooking the Santee River. These outposts now provided protection for supply convoys headed into the interior.

Meanwhile at Mount Joseph, Tom was waiting for permission to travel to Santee, and Harriott was eagerly awaiting his arrival at Hampton plantation. On January 7 Harriott wrote to her mother in Charleston:

> I am extremely anxious to hear from poor Tom, as we have not heard a syllable of him, or any of the family, since the letter you sent me, from him to you; the weather last week was so fine, that I really thought he would have been tempted by it to undertake his voyage, and I have been looking out for him every day. Mr. Motte told Mr. Horry he imagined he would be here in ten days from the time he left town.[19]

Before she could send the letter to her mother, Harriott received one from Eliza who had just gotten a letter from Polly

American Patriot and Successful Rice Planter

Brewton at Mount Joseph. It contained some very sad news: Becky Motte, Rebecca's three-year old daughter, had died. The child may have never fully recovered from the first illness that attacked the party at Mount Joseph, for in mid-September everyone at the plantation was reported to be well — "except poor little Beckey."[20] If the little girl was in a weakened condition and had contracted smallpox, her system may not have been strong enough to fight it. It is not surprising that Polly Brewton undertook the task of writing the letter as Rebecca was no doubt too exhausted from taking care of her daughter and too heartbroken to write herself. Of the six children Rebecca had borne, only three now remained.

Polly's letter also contained the news that Tom had received permission to come to Charleston, not to Santee. Eliza, who had been making her home with the Horry family since the Siege of Charleston, was at the Horry townhouse and told Harriott that she was expecting Tom and his family to arrive there at any time. Daniel Horry, who had taken the oath of allegiance to the king rather than lose his property, had invited Tom and his family to stay at his house in town.

Harriott was very disappointed that Tom was not coming to Santee, but on January 7, she still held out hope that it might happen. She wrote to her mother: "but as I understand that Mr. Motte was to obtain leave for Tom to come to Santee and he [Mr. Motte] had not got home when Mrs. Brewton's letter was wrote, I am still in hopes of seeing them [Tom and his family] here."[21] It is obvious that on January 7, Harriott thought that Jacob Motte, having finished his business in Charleston, had left the area and was on his way back to Mount Joseph.

What happened to him is something of a mystery. He left no will, indicating that his death was sudden, and the site of his burial is unknown. There is a memorial to him in St. Philip's Episcopal Cemetery in Charleston that states that he "departed this life on the 20th day of January, 1781, aged 51." However, he is not buried there. If he had indeed begun his journey back to Mount Joseph, he may have met with an accident on the way or suffered a heart attack or stroke. Tom and his wife and son were at the Horry townhouse in Charleston by January 16.[22] If Jacob Motte died in Charleston, as some sources indicate, then surely his daughter and son-in-law would have had him properly buried at St. Philip's.

It is not known when the melancholy news reached Rebecca that her husband was dead. Unfortunately, dealing with the loss of her husband and her youngest child, were not her only problems. By January, Rebecca and the others had moved from the farmhouse to the newly-built house on the bluff overlooking the Congaree River, and it was there the British suddenly appeared, telling her they were appropriating her new house, fortifying it as an outpost to protect the supply route from Charleston.

Chapter Eight
Fort Motte — Part One

Rebecca was probably surprised when the British showed up on her doorstep announcing they planned to commandeer her house and fortify it. After all, they already had an outpost at nearby Belleville plantation. Belleville, belonging to Colonel William Thomson, former commander of the 3rd South Carolina Regiment, had been appropriated by the British shortly after the fall of Charleston — most likely to send a message to the local residents. It was standard British practice to make an example of local rebel leaders by either detaining them in other parts of the state or seizing their property. As early as June 6, the British were using the plantation as a campsite, but it was not until the late summer or early fall that they decided to fortify the house and use it as an outpost.[1]

Now for some reason, the British high command had decided to abandon the fortification at Belleville and move the outpost to Mount Joseph. As a result, Lieutenant McPherson was at Rebecca's door, accompanied by a troop of some one hundred fifty soldiers — British regulars, Hessian mercenaries, and Tory Provincials.[2] The soldiers immediately fanned out and set up their encampment on the grounds adjacent to the mansion, while the Lieutenant and the rest of the officers took up residence in the house.

McPherson appears by all accounts to have been a pleasant young man who took his military responsibilities very seriously. He may have preferred that Rebecca and the rest of the family move to another location, but it seems he did not insist upon their removal. Perhaps Rebecca expressed a desire to remain. According to Polly Brewton, who recounted her experiences at Mount Joseph to Alexander Garden in 1783, Lieutenant

McPherson "suffered Mrs. Motte and her family to remain and an apartment [room] was allowed for their accommodation."[3] This suggests that Rebecca wanted to continue living in the house, and Lieutenant McPherson yielded to her wishes. With the departure of Betsey, Tom, and the baby, and the deaths that had occurred, there were now only four women and four or five children, plus one or two of their enslaved servants left to share the house with five or six British officers.

Rebecca was always a gracious hostess and, although the British officers were uninvited guests, she would have been courteous to them, even though one of the officers "made it his chief occupation to provoke the ladies of the family by taunts and invectives against their countrymen."[4] Her niece Polly was not so accommodating, and evidently took great pleasure in crossing verbal swords with the British officers. Alexander Garden, obviously much impressed with the high-spirited Polly, wrote: "The liveliness of Mrs. Brewton was very fascinating, and the more liberal and enlightened among the British, who met with very little of wit or intellect, anxiously sought her society."[5] It seems the verbal banter between the "lively Mrs. Brewton" and the British officers was enjoyed by both parties.

While Lieutenant McPherson's men were working hard to enclose the mansion house with a palisade and erect earthen ramparts around it, Lord Cornwallis was preparing to contend with a new American Commander. In October, the Continental Congress had appointed General Nathanael Greene to replace General Gates as the Commander of the Southern Department. In early December, Greene arrived in Charlotte, North Carolina, to assume command of his troops. He immediately reorganized the army, dividing it, and giving command of one-half to General Daniel Morgan. On the 21st of December, Morgan headed west with his troops towards the British outpost at Ninety Six. His orders were "to give protection to that part of the country and spirit up the people" and to annoy the enemy.[6]

American Patriot and Successful Rice Planter

Cornwallis, fearing an American attack on the outpost at Ninety Six, responded by sending his favorite commander, Tarleton, with a force of approximately 1,000 men to stop them. On January 17, 1781, the two armies clashed at a place called Cowpens. General Morgan and his men won a decisive victory there over the hated commander of the British Legion. When the battle was over after just an hour of fighting, almost ninety percent of the British forces were either dead, wounded, or taken prisoner.

After the victory at Cowpens, General Greene joined forces with Daniel Morgan and took the army into North Carolina. Cornwallis followed, for not only did he want to destroy Greene's army, but he also wanted to conquer North Carolina. Annoyed by the actions of Patriot militia who were making life difficult for the British, Cornwallis thought the best way to keep South Carolina under British control was to eliminate North Carolina as a safe haven for Patriot forces. Consequently, for the next six weeks or more, Cornwallis and his army chased General Greene and his army over the state of North Carolina, coming close to catching up, but never quite being able to do so.

Although it appeared that Greene's strategy was one of playing cat-and-mouse with the British, he was not averse to facing Cornwallis in battle, though he wanted it to be at a place and a time of his choosing. On March 15, he decided the time was right, and the place he chose for the confrontation was Guilford Courthouse, a small hamlet in the backcountry of North Carolina. The ensuing battle was the largest and most fiercely contested battle of the American Revolution in the South, and, although it resulted in a tactical victory for the British, the cost was high. Cornwallis lost nearly a third of his army that day. He then decided to take his battered and weary troops to the Carolina coast where they could rest and receive much needed supplies from Charleston by sea. When the army had recovered and was ready to move out, Cornwallis would turn his back on South Carolina and head north to Virginia to face his destiny that fall in Yorktown.

While Greene had been leading Cornwallis and his army all over North Carolina, Partisan forces had been busy harassing the British in South Carolina. On the 19th of February, General Sumter laid siege to Fort Granby, located on the Congaree, some thirty-five miles up-river from Mount Joseph. Upon learning that Rawdon was approaching at the head of a large relief force, Sumter was forced to call off the siege on the 21st and retreat downriver to look for another British outpost to attack. He chose Belleville.

Arriving at Colonel Thomson's plantation on February 22, Sumter's men charged across an open field to attack the outpost, getting close enough to the fortifications to set fire to some of the outbuildings before being driven back. The fighting didn't last long — only about half an hour — but the sounds of the attack must have caused alarm among the women and children at Mount Joseph. Sumter then retreated downriver to set up camp at Manigault's Ferry, leaving a few men behind to harass the British and keep an eye on their activities. Meanwhile, the work at Mount Joseph continued, and by the end of March it was nearly finished. On April 7, Sumter, whose spies had kept him apprised of the situation at Belleville, reported to General Greene: "Post at Co Thompson's is Broke up & the Troops Removed to the Congarees."[7] The fortifications at Mount Joseph were now complete.

Rebecca's house was a large, two or three-story building. The British had surrounded the house and a small open area on its east side with a high wooden palisade rising nine feet from the ground, with a gate located in the southeast corner. Blockhouses with loopholes to allow soldiers to fire at attackers had been built into two opposite corners of the palisade wall. On the outside was an earthen rampart or embankment ten to eleven feet wide. A seven-and-a-half foot wide, six feet deep ditch ran in front of the rampart. As if those were not deterrents enough, about twenty to thirty feet from the ditch was an abatis

— a barrier made of felled trees placed so their branches faced outward toward an attacking force.[8] It was a formidable sight. When General Marion first saw it, he described it as "obstinate and strong." The British called it Fort Motte.

Now that the fort was complete, McPherson would have been anxious to have the civilians removed to another location. He would have explained to Rebecca that there was a good possibility that the Americans might attack Fort Motte as they had Belleville earlier in the year, and he not only advised the "immediate removal" of the entire family but "insisted" on it.[9] Rebecca likely readily agreed — it would be unthinkable for them to remain inside the fort if there were any chance it would come under attack.

Rebecca packed up her household, and she and the others moved back to the farmhouse they had previously occupied. According to Polly Brewton, when the ladies were leaving the mansion house, she spotted a quiver of arrows, which she described as a "novelty given to Jacob Motte by a favorite African."[10] "I will take these with me," she is reported to have said, "to prevent their destruction by the soldiers." As the ladies were passing through the gate of the fort to travel to their new home, Polly recounted, McPherson stopped her and, drawing forth one of the arrows from the quiver she was carrying, pressed his finger to the point and asked, "What have you there, Mrs. B?" "For God's sake, Major, be careful," she is said to have replied, "these arrows are poisoned."[11]

General Greene had been shadowing Cornwallis as he moved his troops to the coast after the Battle of Guilford Courthouse. However, at Ramsey's Mill in North Carolina, the American commander halted his pursuit. He was not planning to follow Cornwallis any further — instead, he was going to take his army south to re-take South Carolina and Georgia. Anxious to give Cornwallis the impression that the American army was still pursuing him, Greene sent one of his favorite young commanders to harass Cornwallis's rear guard and act as a decoy while the rest of the army marched south.

The man he chose for this mission was Lt. Colonel Henry Lee, III, a Virginian and an outstanding military leader who had earned the respect of George Washington early in the war. Lee, who had been given the nickname "Light Horse Harry" because of his superb horsemanship, commanded a unit of about 300 men composed of equal numbers of infantry and cavalry. It was known as Lee's Legion, and its members wore short green jackets and buff or white colored pants — much like the uniforms worn by the British Legion.

On April 6, Lee led his troops eastward from Ramsey's Mill while Greene marched his army south to re-enter South Carolina. In Greene's absence, Partisan forces had been doing an excellent job of controlling the countryside, discouraging Loyalist support, disrupting British supply lines, gathering intelligence, and in general harassing British troops. While these were all important missions, Greene knew that if he were going to drive the British out of the South, it would be necessary for the militia and the Continental Army to work together as they had at Cowpens. With that end in view, Greene had given Lee instructions that when he completed his mission, he was to return to South Carolina and, with Partisan militia, attack the British outposts on the Santee. On April 14, Light Horse Harry Lee rode into Francis Marion's camp.

The timing could not have been better. Marion was weary and in low spirits. He had spent the entire month of March in a series of running battles with the British. Lord Rawdon, in an attempt to drive Marion out of the eastern part of South Carolina, had sent Lt. Colonel Watson east along the Santee River, while Lt. Colonel Doyle and his men marched south from Camden. The goal was for Doyle to try to come up behind Marion and trap him between the two British columns.

American Patriot and Successful Rice Planter

Doyle was not able to do so, and Marion was left free to concentrate his efforts on Watson — inflicting such severe casualties on his troops that the British commander was forced to seek refuge in Georgetown. Unfortunately, while Marion was engaged with Watson, Doyle had found and destroyed his base camp on Snow Island. All of Marion's provisions, supplies, and ammunition had been stored there. It was a devastating loss.

Marion's men were militia and came and went as they pleased. He was often frustrated by the fact that he never knew how many men he would have available at any given time. Now it was April and time for farmers to begin to sow their seed, and some of his men were slipping quietly away to return home for the spring planting. Consequently, Marion was sitting in camp with a depleted force, short of ammunition and provisions, and weary from a month of constant campaigning. To make matters worse, he had just gotten word that Watson had marched out of Georgetown and was moving toward him. He was thoroughly discouraged. Then, Light Horse Harry Lee rode into his camp and everything changed.

Lee and Marion were well acquainted, having campaigned successfully together in 1780 before Lee had been recalled to the Continental army. They would have greeted each other warmly. The arrival of Lee's Legion would have lifted not only Marion's spirits but the spirits of his men as well, and they would have all listened intently as Lee conveyed Greene's instructions: together they were to attack the British outposts guarding the supply and communication routes between Charleston and the backcountry, and they were to start with Fort Watson. The next day the combined forces of Marion and Lee, some 420 strong, rode out to lay siege to Fort Watson, located on the Santee River downstream from Fort Motte.

Fort Watson was commanded by Lieutenant James McKay who had only a force of 114 men — the defenders quite outnumbered by their attackers. Still, Fort Watson was well fortified. It stood on top of an Indian mound approximately 30 feet high, with stockade walls about six or seven feet high. At the base of the mound were three rows of abatis, and in front of the abatis was a ditch. The land around the mound was clear — there were no trees to give the Patriots cover.

It was a daunting sight, and without artillery — which Marion and Lee did not have — taking the fort would be a challenge. Sumter had certainly found it to be so when he tried and failed to capture it earlier. Knowing that with just one piece of artillery, the task would be much easier, Lee wrote to Greene requesting that a field piece be sent to them immediately. Unfortunately, Greene was moving towards Rawdon at Camden and was unable to spare the men to bring them one of his six-pounders.

Without artillery, the only course left open to the Americans was to try to force the British to surrender by cutting off the water supply to the fort. But the British foiled their attempts to do so, leaving them in a quandary. At this point, Major Hezekiah Maham, one of Marion's officers, offered a suggestion: build a wooden tower high enough for men to be able to fire down on the defenders inside the fort. The plan was adopted, and work on the project started immediately. It was finished by April 23. It was "a large, strong, oblong pen ... covered on the top with a floor of logs and protected on the side opposite to the fort with a breastwork of light timber."[12] Riflemen immediately climbed to the platform on the top and began firing on the British soldiers in the fort. Meanwhile, Marion's men, supported by Lee's infantry, entered the ditch surrounding the abatis and began to pull it apart in preparation for storming the walls. The fire from the riflemen was deadly, and Lieutenant McKay was finally forced to surrender. Inside the fort, the Americans found a pleasant surprise: a much-needed large store of provisions, ammunition, and other supplies.

The day after the fall of Fort Watson, General Greene wrote Marion a well-deserved letter of thanks for his services. The let-

American Patriot and Successful Rice Planter

ter surely must have pleased Marion, but what probably pleased him even more was Greene's promise to send him a field piece, along with an adequate supply of powder and shot. Before they marched off to take the next outpost, though, Greene had another job for Marion and Lee. Marion's nemesis, Lt. Colonel Watson, was marching from the east to join forces with Rawdon in Camden, and Greene wanted Marion and Lee to intercept him. Not knowing for sure which route Watson would take, the American leaders decided to wait for him on the north side of the Santee close to Manigault's Ferry.

Somehow, Watson managed to elude them, and the disappointed Americans turned their attention back to the goal of capturing Fort Motte. By this time, the artillery piece had arrived, and on the morning of May 6 with the six-pounder in tow, Marion and Lee crossed the Santee and made their way to nearby Belleville plantation, the home of Patriot leader Colonel William Thomson. Standing on Buckhead Hill, only a mile or two to the southeast of Fort Motte, Belleville was strategically placed, and the Americans were probably hoping to use the site as their base camp during their assault on the fort.

Thomson was at home when Marion and Lee rode up to his house that May morning. After the fall of Charleston, he had spent several months in town as a prisoner of war before being been paroled to his home. In fact, he had been at Belleville in February when his British-held plantation had been attacked by Sumter.[13] He would have given Marion and Lee a warm welcome — and some vital information about the fort and its defenders.

Fort Motte was an important post for the British. It was the repository of supplies coming from Charleston intended for Camden, Fort Granby, Orangeburg, and even far-distant Ninety Six; without it the British would be hard-pressed to maintain their garrisons in the backcountry. Rebecca and the ladies at the farmhouse would have witnessed the arrival of numerous convoys, and been used to the sounds of horses and wagons coming and going. Early on the morning of May 6, a small detachment of dragoons guarding supplies intended for Camden was making their way up the steep road to the fort.

At ten o'clock that same morning, Levi Smith left Fort Motte to make the 200-yard walk to his home for breakfast. Smith, a Tory, had owned a store on the north side of the Congaree near McCord's Ferry until Patriot raids compelled him to move his family to the other side of the river, close to Fort Motte. Already a Justice of the Peace under the British government, in February, Levi had agreed to gather information about General Sumter and other Partisan leaders for Rawdon. Lieutenant McPherson had then asked him to take command of the 45 Loyalist volunteers at Fort Motte. As he was walking home that morning, completely unaware of any danger, he suddenly found himself accosted by a party of Lee's cavalry. They took him prisoner and marched him to Belleville plantation about one mile away where, to his great shock, he found the combined troops of Marion and Lee along with the two American commanders.[14]

It might have been Thomson who then told Marion about another strategic location he should occupy — a farmhouse located on a ridge a few hundred yards north of the fort. This farmhouse, he would also have mentioned, was the residence of Rebecca Motte, an ardent Patriot, and several female members of her family. Marion and Lee would have made their way immediately over to the ridge to reconnoiter the area and make themselves known to the occupants of the house.

The chances are very good that Marion and Rebecca were already acquainted as they both came from the Santee area. Therefore, it was probably Marion who greeted Rebecca and explained to her that they had come to lay siege to Fort Motte — a mission that would have met with her sincere approval. Then, he most likely introduced Rebecca to Colonel Lee who, no doubt, greeted her and the other ladies with all the charm and grace of a true Virginia gentleman.

American Patriot and Successful Rice Planter

From the ridge in front of the farmhouse, Marion and Lee could look out across the ravine to Fort Motte standing tall and strong in the distance. As they stood surveying the landscape, the two leaders must have realized they were facing yet another serious challenge. Their first step was to surround the fort.

It was decided that Marion and his men would occupy the area near Belleville to the southeast of the fort, while Colonel Lee and his troops were to camp in the vicinity of the farmhouse. The soldiers spread out, occupying several areas around the fort, anywhere from two hundred to three hundred yards from its walls.[15] Rebecca was probably delighted to have Colonel Lee's men camping around her house, and with her customary generosity and graciousness, invited Lee to make his quarters inside the house — an invitation he readily accepted.

Marion and Lee then began preparations for capturing the fort. They planned to have a sap (or approach trench) dug toward the north wall of the fort. It would begin at the ravine some 400 yards from the fort and be dug in a zig-zag manner to keep the enemy from firing down a straight pathway at the workers. To the east of the fort, a mound of earth was to be formed upon which Captain Finley, who had brought the six-pounder, would place his artillery piece.

The plan for taking the fort was simple. The trench was to be dug as close as possible to the abatis. Then Lee's infantry, with bayonets fixed, would rush the fort from the sap. The artillery piece would rake the fort's north palisade to keep the defenders off the wall while the attack was in progress. While the sap was being dug, Marion would station his riflemen in a position to keep the defenders from shooting at the workers. Fortunately, the British at Fort Motte had no useable artillery.[16]

Siege warfare was slow and meticulous, and while the digging of the sap was hard work, it was also very dull. However, the tedium was alleviated by Rebecca's hospitality — which seems to have been extended to all. Lee wrote glowingly of her generosity:

> Encamping contiguous to Mrs. Motte's dwelling, this officer had, upon his arrival, been requested in the most pressing terms to make her house his quarters. The invitation was accordingly accepted; and not only the lieutenant-colonel, but every officer of his corps, off duty, daily experienced her liberal hospitality, politely proffered, and as politely administered. Nor was the attention of this amiable lady confined to that class of war which never fail to attract attention. While her richly-spread table presented with taste and fashion all the luxuries of her opulent country, and her sideboard offered without reserve the best wines of Europe — antiquated relics of happier days — her active benevolence found its way to the sick and to the wounded; cherishing with softest kindness infirmity and misfortunes, converting despair into hope, and nursing debility into strength.[17]

In addition to Rebecca's hospitality, some of Lee's officers undoubtedly found the tedium of siege warfare lessened by the society of the young ladies in the group — Polly Brewton who was in her mid-twenties, Fanny Motte almost eighteen, and Mary Motte who was thirteen. The poet Alfred, Lord Tennyson once wrote: "In the Spring a young man's fancy lightly turns to thoughts of love." Young John Middleton, one of Lee's officers, found his thoughts turning in that direction — for two years later he and Fanny were married.

Meanwhile, the hard work continued. Relays of men worked four hours at a time, and with the help of enslaved workers from Mount Joseph, Belleville, and other nearby plantations, the digging of the sap progressed rapidly. By May 10, it was close enough to the fort for Marion and Lee to ask Lieutenant McPherson to surrender — as was usual in siege warfare. McPherson replied that, "he should continue to resist to the last moment."[18]

At some point during that day, Marion learned that Rawdon was abandoning Camden. At first, he thought it might just be a large foraging party heading out from town, but a courier arrived during the night with a message from General Greene, confirming that Rawdon was retreating. He urged them to redouble their efforts to take the fort, and Marion and Lee pressed the men to continue working on the sap through the night of May 11. On this night, Lee reported that, from the ridge, Rawdon's campfires could be seen glowing in the distance.[19]

Marion and Lee knew they had to act quickly before Rawdon's relief forces arrived. The space inside Fort Motte was not large, as the British had built the palisade walls only a few feet from the house on three sides, leaving a small open plaza on the east side. With the addition of the dragoons who had arrived on the morning of May 6, there were now approximately one hundred eighty-four men crammed inside the fort.[20] If the Americans could set fire to the house, the British must either surrender or be burned alive.

Lee wrote: "persuaded that our ditch [sap] would be within arrow-shot before noon of the next day, Marion and Lee determined to adopt this speedy mode of effecting their object." He continued that "orders were instantly issued to prepare bows and arrows with missive combustible matter." However, it was with great reluctance that both Marion and Lee ordered the burning of Rebecca's house. Destruction of private property was "repugnant to their principles," especially the property of a staunch Patriot. Lee's men who had benefited from Rebecca's hospitality during the siege were also troubled by the thought of burning her house.[21]

However, the fort must be taken before Rawdon arrived. In his memoirs, Lee wrote that he was the one who approached Rebecca and told her they were going to have to set her house on fire, while other sources indicate that it was both Marion and Lee who spoke to her. Since Marion was the commanding officer, it is reasonable to assume that, if he did not tell her their plans himself, he was at least present when she found out. Rebecca's response varies slightly with the different accounts of the incident — but the gist of it is always the same. According to Lee: "With a smile of complacency this exemplary lady listened to the embarrassed officer, and gave instant relief to his agitated feelings, by declaring that she was gratified with the opportunity of contributing to the good of her country, and that she would view the approaching scene with delight."[22]

Marion and Lee would both have been greatly relieved to find that Rebecca was in favor of it. It was probably at this point that Rebecca remembered the quiver of arrows that Polly had rescued from the mansion house and that she had "hidden away on the topmost shelf of her wardrobe." She asked the two men to wait for a moment — she had something she thought might facilitate their mission.[23]

Chapter Nine
Fort Motte — Part Two

In 1855, when she was an old woman, Harriott Horry Rutledge, the daughter of Harriott and Daniel Horry, wrote her recollections of the exciting story Rebecca used to tell of "setting her own house on fire." She had heard the story so many times as a child, Harriot recounted, that she could still picture Rebecca hurrying into the farmhouse, dragging a low stool to the front of her wardrobe, and standing on it to search the top shelf for the quiver of arrows. When she found it, Harriott wrote, Rebecca took the arrows out of their case and handed them down to Fanny to take to Marion and Lee, who were waiting patiently outside.[1] The two men had not known what to expect. They had been planning to use flaming arrows shot from bows to ignite the roof of the house and must have wondered what Rebecca could possess that would be more effective. As Lee took the handful of arrows from Fanny, Rebecca was said to have explained that the arrows were special fire arrows, designed to be used with a musket.[2]

Musket arrows, as they were called, were unusual at this time, but they were not unknown. In the previous century, they had been used to good advantage during the English Civil Wars and were described by one 17th-Century historian as being "good either for service on sea to burne the sailes of ships, or on land for disordering men..."[3] Because of their effectiveness at sea, they were probably still being used in the 18th century aboard some merchant ships as a defense against privateers, and Marion and Lee may very well have been familiar with them.

Musket arrows were also used during the Siege of Ninety Six at the end of May. According to Lieutenant Roderick Mackenzie, a British officer present at the siege, "African arrows were thrown by the besiegers on the roofs of the British barracks to set them on fire, but this design was immediately counteracted by Lieut. Col. Cruger..." The footnote to this sentence reads:

> These were arrows fitted to the bore of musquets from which they were discharged. They were entwined with flax, dipped in combustibles lighted, and armed at the end with a barbed spear. Captain McPherson of Delancey's had defended Fort Motte with admirable gallantry, but his barracks being set on fire by these arrows, he was compelled to surrender.[4]

Gratefully, the two American leaders took the arrows and returned to their troops. As soon as their men were in position, the Americans gave the British one last opportunity to surrender. Doctor Matthew Irvine, a courier in Lee's legion, was sent to the fort with a flag of truce. He explained to Lieutenant McPherson that the Americans were in position to set fire to the house and it would be prudent for him to surrender. However, the defenders had somehow received word the day before that Rawdon was marching to their rescue, and even though Doctor Irvine explained that the British commander had not as yet crossed the Santee and was in no position to relieve the fort, Lieutenant McPherson reiterated his intention to hold out to the last.

It was almost noon when Dr. Irvine returned and the rays of the sun had dried out the shingles on the roof of Rebecca's house, making them easier to ignite.[5] There are different accounts of what happened next; all seem to agree that two or three arrows were fired at the roof of the house. Lee wrote that the first arrow; "struck and communicated its fire; a second was shot at another quarter of the roof, and a third at a third quarter; this last also took effect; and like the first, soon kindled a blaze."[6] However, Charles Cotesworth Pinckney, II, Rebecca's grandson, in recounting what his grandmother had told him about the incident said, "the first two did not ignite; the third set the roof on fire."[7] Polly Brewton gave another account. She told Alexander Garden that afterwards they were told that the first arrow "had missed its aim and fell at the feet of Lieutenant McPherson" and it was the second arrow that set fire to the roof.[8]

No matter how it happened, the roof of the house was set on fire, and when British soldiers rushed onto the roof to remove the burning shingles, they came under fire from Marion's sharpshooters and Captain Finley's artillery crew and quickly retreated back inside the house. At this point, Lieutenant McPherson had no choice but to raise the white flag and surrender. According to Pinckney: "The Americans rushed in; extinguished the fire, and saved the house — an act of gratitude to the owner for her patriotic devotion."[9]

Following the protocol of the times, the British regulars surrendered to Colonel Lee of the Continental army while the Loyalist volunteers surrendered to General Marion, the militia commander. All the British prisoners, except for the officers, were then marched off to Colonel Thomson's mill house, which stood at the bottom of Buckhead Hill. The number of prisoners was reported to be 184 men — British regulars, Hessians and Tory Provincials.[10]

It is hard to imagine Rebecca's feelings as she and the others stood on the ridge watching the assault on Fort Motte. From the distance it would have been difficult for them to determine exactly what was happening, but they would have been watching intently for smoke rising from the fort — a sign that the attackers had been able to set fire to the house. A messenger was probably dispatched to the farmhouse soon after the surrender to inform Rebecca that, although the roof had caught fire, the flames had been safely extinguished. It must have been an incredible relief to her.

By this time, it was early afternoon, and the ladies at the farmhouse would have been preparing for dinner — in the 18th century, people ate their main meal of the day between two and four o'clock. Rebecca would have assumed that Lee and his officers would be returning to take dinner with them as

Rebecca Brewton Motte

was their practice, and in a spirit of generosity, she decided to invite all the officers — Continentals, militia, and British — to dine with them.

According to Lee: "McPherson and his officers accompanied their captors to Mrs. Motte's and partook with them of a sumptuous dinner; soothing in the sweets of social intercourse the ire which the preceding conflict had engendered." He then continued:

> The deportment and demeanor of Mrs. Motte gave a zest to the pleasures of the table. She did the honors with that unaffected politeness which ever excites esteem, mingled with admiration. Conversing with ease, vivacity, and good sense, she obliterated our recollections of the injury she had received; and though warmly attached to the defenders of her country, the engaging amiability of her manners, left it doubtful which set of officers constituted these defenders.[11]

It would not have been in Rebecca's nature to have been discourteous to anyone — even the enemies of her country.

While the American and British officers were enjoying Rebecca's hospitality, a different drama was beginning at the mill house where the Loyalists and British regulars were being held. Levi Smith, who had been a prisoner since the beginning of the siege, was among those confined in the mill house and he later recounted his experiences at Fort Motte in a letter to *The Royal Gazette*. Around sunset, he reported, one of Colonel Lee's men appeared at the door asking for Lieutenant Fulker, an officer in the Loyalist militia. He had orders, he announced, to take Fulker to the fort to be hanged — he had been accused of causing the death of a Patriot woman by turning her out of her house while she was recovering from smallpox. Fulker begged to be brought to trial so he could plead his innocence, but his request was refused and he was taken away.[12]

In the 18th century, a person condemned to be hanged was placed on a stool, the top of a ladder, on the back of a horse, or the back of a cart, while a noose tied at the end of a rope suspended from an overhead beam or tree branch was put around his or her neck. Whatever was supporting the prisoner was then removed and the condemned was left dangling from the beam. The weight of the body caused the noose to tighten around the neck and the person was slowly strangled. It could take anywhere from ten to twenty minutes for death to occur. Lieutenant Fulker was hauled off to the fort and hanged from the overhead beam of the palisade gate.

After a while, according to Levi, the same messenger returned to the mill house and asked for John Jackson, a private in the militia. He was accused of carrying express messages for the British and killing one of Sumter's men in February during the American attack on Belleville plantation. He, too, pleaded for a trial but to no purpose. He was subsequently taken to the fort and hanged.[13]

It was dark by this time, and no more messengers appeared at the door, leaving the prisoners undisturbed for the night. Levi was not at all uneasy, for although two men had been taken away and executed, he felt no alarm for his own safety. During the early days of his captivity, it had been agreed that he would be exchanged for Samuel Cooper, the brother of Lieutenant William Cooper, one of Marion's officers. Samuel had been captured by Doyle in the raid on Marion's camp on Snow Island and was now a prisoner with Rawdon.[14]

Early the next morning, Levi reported, the same messenger appeared at the door of the mill house asking for Hugh Maskelly. He was accused of serving as a guide for Colonel Doyle and disclosing to the British where the Patriots in the neighborhood had hidden their valuables. He had no sooner been taken away than a sergeant and two privates of the Continental army arrived looking for Levi Smith. He was accused of being a Justice of the Peace and a militia officer under the crown and of being responsible for the burning of Mrs. Mc-

Rebecca Brewton Motte

Cord's house. They had orders, the sergeant announced, to take him to the fort for hanging.[15]

Levi was stunned. He had been expecting his name to be called so he could join the British officers who were leaving that morning for Nelson's Ferry where the exchange for Samuel Cooper would take place. What he was not expecting was to be called to the fort to be hanged. His protests and cries that he was to be exchanged fell on deaf ears. He pleaded with the soldiers to at least tell his wife and children what was happening and have them come to say their goodbyes.

By the time Levi and his guards reached the fort, the British officers who were preparing to leave for Nelson's Ferry were gathered outside, along with some of the Continental officers. Levi's wife and children had also made their appearance but were forced to stay some distance away. Maskelly was not yet dead, and as there was no other rope available to hang Levi, his execution was momentarily delayed. At this point, the British officers began to protest the hanging. British militia officers were the same as regular officers, Lieutenant McPherson told the men, and any injury to Levi Smith would be looked upon as having been done to one of them. There would be repercussions. One of the Continental officers said: "It is a shame to take the life of any man without a trial. This man, let him be a devil, or what he will, ought to have a trial."[16]

The protests fell on deaf ears, and since Maskelly was now dead, preparations were being made to hang Smith. Suddenly, a commotion was heard and General Marion appeared on horseback with his sword drawn.

> He asked, in a passion, what they were doing there? The soldiers answered, "We are hanging them people, Sir!" He then asked them, who ordered them to hang any person? They replied, Col. Lee. "I will let you know, damn you," replied Marion, "that I command here and not Col. Lee. Do you know, that if you hang this man, Lord Rawdon will

American Patriot and Successful Rice Planter

hang a good man in his place; that he will hang Sam Cooper, who is to be exchanged for him?"[17]

Levi was taken back to the mill house. He did not know it at the time, but he owed his life to William Cooper, who had seen the soldiers taking him to the fort and hurried off in search of Marion. Cooper was worried about the consequences to his brother if Smith were hanged.[18]

Smith's account of his experiences at Fort Motte is certainly credible, and while there seems to be little reason to doubt his story, his claim that Lee ordered the executions of the four Tories does require closer scrutiny. It was not the policy of the Continental Army to execute prisoners of war without a trial, and such acts would certainly have been condemned by General Greene. It seems unlikely that Lee, a high-ranking officer who considered himself a man of honor, would have deliberately violated that policy. Moreover, the Loyalists surrendered to the militia, not the Continental Army, and so were Francis Marion's responsibility, not Lee's.

In his memoirs, Lee only mentioned the attempted hanging of Levi Smith and not the hangings of the three other prisoners. He wrote:

> The commandant, with the regulars...were taken possession of by Lee; while the loyalists were delivered to Marion. Among the latter was a Mr. Smith, who had been charged with burning the houses of his neighbors friendly to their country. This man consequently became very obnoxious, and his punishment was loudly demanded by many of the militia serving under the brigadier; but the humanity of Marion could not be overcome. Smith was secured from his surrounding enemies... and taken under the general's protection.[19]

Lee clearly blamed the attempted hanging of Levi Smith on the militia, and they would have certainly had strong motives for wanting to hang him. They would also have had strong motives for wanting to hang the other three Tories as, in their opinion, these men had committed equally egregious acts against

Patriots. Whether Lee would have found these acts flagrant enough to order the summary executions of the offenders is another matter.

If Lee did not order the hangings, then, who did issue the order? It is possible that no one did. The most likely scenario is that while, Lee and Marion were having dinner with the other officers, a group of soldiers allowed their desire for revenge to get the better of their judgement, and the hangings began. Members of the militia were most likely involved, as they would have had the strongest motives, but some Continental soldiers also joined them. A Continental Army veteran from North Carolina stated in his pension application that he had been at Fort Motte during the siege and had been taking part in the execution of prisoners until Marion "ordered us not to hang any more of the Tories."[20]

In the meantime, what had happened to Lord Rawdon? He had been on his way to Fort Motte, but he was not able to march directly there, as he couldn't cross the river at McCord's Ferry with the Americans encamped just on the other side. Instead, he had to make the long trip to Nelson's Ferry where there was a British outpost to protect his crossing. By the time he crossed the river, it was May 14, and he discovered that Fort Motte had fallen. Still, he was determined to go after Marion and Lee and started to make his way to the fort when he received intelligence that Greene had crossed at McCord's Ferry and was traveling toward Orangeburg. He decided to turn back.

Unfortunately for him, Rawdon's spies had not given him accurate information. They had mistaken Sumter and his militia for General Greene's troops. Greene had indeed crossed at McCord's Ferry, but he was only accompanied by a small escort. He had come to Fort Motte to talk to one of his most valuable assets — Francis Marion — who had expressed the alarming intention of leaving South Carolina and offering his services to the army in the north.

American Patriot and Successful Rice Planter

Greene arrived at the site soon after the surrender, in time to exchange greetings with the captured British officers and compliment Lieutenant McPherson on his gallant defense of the fort.[21] He then set up camp at nearby McCord's Ferry. It was there that he had a long, private conversation with Marion. It was the first time the two men had ever met. What passed between them is not known, but whatever was said must have been satisfying to Marion, for after his talk with General Greene, he never mentioned leaving the South again.

After all the excitement, life slowly returned to normal at Mount Joseph. The palisade around the house came down, the ditches were filled in and leveled off, and damages to the house repaired. The soldiers dispersed to fight other battles in other places — Lee to Fort Granby and Marion to Georgetown. Greene spent two days at McCord's Ferry writing letters to General Washington and the president of the Continental Congress, outlining the events of the last two weeks — especially the victories at Fort Watson and Fort Motte. Then he, too, left.

It was a slightly diminished group that took up residence once again in the house at Mount Joseph. Polly was anxious to return to Charleston, and when she heard that Major Hyrne would soon be going into town, she applied for and received permission to travel with him.[22] Hyrne had been appointed the new deputy commissioner for the exchange of prisoners, and was about to leave for Charleston to begin negotiations with the British. The major and Polly left soon after the surrender of Fort Motte. With Polly's departure, only Rebecca, her two daughters, her sister-in-law and her children, along with their enslaved servants, remained out of the large group that had traveled from Fairfield to Mount Joseph less than a year before.

The course of the war had changed radically during the time Rebecca and her family had been at Mount Joseph. Charleston had surrendered only a year earlier, leaving the Patriots too stunned and cowed to resist, as the British fanned out over the countryside and took control of the rest of the state. Gradually, Patriots had ceased to be intimidated, and opposition to British rule grew and, as a consequence of the combined efforts of Partisan fighters and the Continental Army, the British had been forced to relinquish most of what they had gained.

On May 10, Rawdon abandoned Camden, and the next day Sumter captured the British outpost at Orangeburg. Marion and Lee took Fort Motte on May 12, and Lee had gone on to capture Fort Granby, the last of the supply outposts, on May 15. One year after the fall of Charleston, the British held only Charleston and Georgetown on the coast and Ninety Six in the backcountry. When the irrepressible Polly arrived in Charleston, she was met by a British officer who asked her rather anxiously, "What was the news in the country?" To which she replied, "That all nature smiled, for everything was *Greene* to Monck's Corner."[23]

While the British were able to hold on to Charleston, they could not keep Georgetown and Ninety Six. Greene began his Siege of Ninety Six on May 22, and Marion captured Georgetown on the 28th. Unfortunately, Lord Rawdon immediately left Charleston to march to the relief of the fort, and Greene had to call off the siege on June 19. However, without the supply outposts, the British position at Ninety Six was untenable, and, on July 8, the troops stationed there abandoned the fort, destroying as much of it as they could before leaving. As the long, hot days of summer set in, Rebecca must have hoped for a period of peace and quiet in which to recover from the upheavals of the previous year. However, she would not be able to rest easy just yet for, despite the gains the Americans had made, the war was far from over. There was still a British army in the field, and Loyalist militia remained active in the backcountry.

In late June, Rebecca received some disturbing news. The negotiations for an exchange of prisoners with the British had been dragging on for weeks, until finally an agreement was reached on June 22. Three days later, Colonel Nisbet Balfour, the British commandant in Charleston, announced that all paroled American officers were to proceed as soon as possible to Philadelphia and remain there until their exchanges had been arranged. Annoyed by the continued resistance of many South Carolinians to British rule, Balfour decided to rid the state of as many ardent supporters of the Patriot cause as possible. Therefore, it was not only the paroled officers who were ordered to leave, but also their families and the families of Patriots who had willingly or unwillingly left the state — an estimated six hundred seventy men, women, and children along with their enslaved servants.[24] The deadline for their departure was August 1. Tom, Betsey, and the baby were among those who would be exiled to Philadelphia, as was Polly Brewton. Evidently, not all British officers found Polly's sharp wit entertaining.[25]

Rebecca would have been very distressed to learn that her daughter, son-in-law, niece, and only grandchild were being sent to Philadelphia. Betsey was expecting her second child in October, and Rebecca would have wanted to be with her when she gave birth — always a dangerous time for both mother and baby. Tom and his injured leg, of course, would always be of concern to her, as would be the well-being of her little grandson. Then there was the voyage itself. She could not have helped remembering her brother's ill-fated voyage to Philadelphia just six years before.

In the middle of July, the two Pinckney brothers, their wives, children, and several enslaved servants set sail for Philadelphia, reaching their destination on the 25th. Rebecca was greatly relieved to learn that Tom, Betsey, and little Tom had all arrived in good health.[26] It appeared she did not need to worry, either, about Betsey being among strangers in Philadelphia. The two Pinckney brothers and their families were to share a house in Germantown, some ten miles from Philadelphia, with Edward (Ned) Rutledge and his family. Charles Cotesworth Pinckney and Ned had married sisters — two of Henry Middleton's daughters — and so were brothers-in-law.

General Greene had been keeping an eye on the relief force under Lord Rawdon as it marched out of Ninety Six, apparently headed for the Congarees. He was anxious to engage Rawdon in battle and thought the opportunity had arisen when his scouts reported that Rawdon was at Orangeburg — a small town located on the north fork of the Edisto River some twenty miles south of Mount Joseph. However, when he arrived on the scene, Greene found the British position too strong to make an attack feasible.

It was now July and the heat and humidity were taking a toll on his army. His Continentals had been on the move since the Battle of Guilford Courthouse in mid-March, and Greene decided it was time to give his weary troops a rest. He moved to the High Hills of Santee — a long hilly region lying north of the Santee River, east of the Wateree River, and stretching for some twenty miles south of Camden. It was a perfect place to establish his headquarters: grain was plentiful in the area, the water was good, and the higher elevation meant cooler temperatures and lower humidity.

In early August, Greene was joined at his headquarters by John Rutledge, the exiled governor of South Carolina. Rutledge had just come from Philadelphia where a situation was developing that put everything Americans had been fighting for in jeopardy. The European powers were growing tired of the war, and in hopes of ending the conflict, had made a proposition to the warring parties. A truce would be called, during which Joseph II of Austria and Catherine the Great of Russia would act as mediators to arrange a permanent peace. The British had reacted favorably to the suggestion, and it was expected that France and Spain, France's new ally, would also agree to it.

The sticking point for the Americans was the fact that the truce would be based on a principle of international law known as *uti possidetis* (as you possess), which meant that each side would keep all the territory it held when the truce began. Under this provision, Great Britain could technically claim all of South Carolina and Georgia in any treaty that was subsequently drawn up — a prospect that was completely unacceptable to the Americans, especially Rutledge and Greene.

Both men felt their best option was to take a two-fold approach: one, drive the British from the territory they now possessed and two, establish civil governments in both states to show the world that Americans governed and controlled these areas. Greene had already set Georgians on the path to establishing civil government in their state, and Rutledge had returned home to do the same in South Carolina. Greene then had the task of driving the British out of the southeast or at least confining them to a small area on the coast.

In pursuing his mission, Greene would be facing a new adversary: Lt. Colonel Alexander Stewart, newly arrived from Great Britain. He was replacing Lord Rawdon, who had been suffering for weeks from malaria and was now on his way back to England to recover his health. Stewart made the first move. On August 3, he seized McCord's Ferry; any thought Rebecca had of continued peace and quiet at Mount Joseph vanished as 1,500 British troops descended on Belleville plantation and encamped there for the better part of the month. Since the British force was so large, it is possible that their encampment may have spilled over onto part of Mount Joseph. However, even if they did not camp on Rebecca's property, British foraging parties would have frequently called at the house looking for provisions and other supplies.

Greene broke camp on August 23, ready to carry out his goal to eliminate the last British army remaining in the field. He marched north from the High Hills of Santee to Camden, hoping much-needed supplies for his poorly equipped army might have arrived there from the north. An eighteenth-century army on the march was a long, cumbersome, slow-moving procession of columns of soldiers, followed by a baggage train — a long string of wagons carrying provisions, tents, ammunition, and other supplies, plus the personal belongings of the officers. Tagging along with the baggage train were women and children, the families of some of the soldiers.

The women, known as "women of the army," were an official part of the army and subject to the same rules and regulations as the soldiers — and the same punishments if they broke those rules. They received half-rations for performing various tasks, the most important of which was taking care of the sick and wounded. Greene probably wanted to reduce the number of noncombatants in his army, for at Camden he ordered the "sick and lame" to remain there and also ordered that "a Sufficient number of Women, particularly those that have Children must be left as Nurses."[27]

From Camden, Greene's army marched to Howell's Ferry and crossed the Congaree, hoping to meet Stewart at Belleville — only to discover that he had left. Stewart, running short of provisions, had moved his army to Eutaw Springs to be nearer the supply trains coming from Charleston.[28] Disappointed at not finding his quarry, Greene camped for a few days at Mount Joseph. John Rutledge had been travelling with him, and no doubt Rebecca, pleased to have the American army on her property instead of the British, treated Rutledge, Greene, and his officers to the same gracious hospitality that had so captivated Colonel Lee.

When Greene left to follow the British army a few days later, John Rutledge remained at Mount Joseph. He had been in ill health since leaving Philadelphia and, no doubt enjoyed spending a few days relaxing at Rebecca's house. They were most likely already acquainted and would have had much in common. John's younger brother Edward was sharing a house with Tom and Betsey in Philadelphia, and as Rutledge had just come from there, he would have been able to give Rebecca the latest news about the family.

On September 8, Greene was granted the confrontation with the British that he had been seeking. The ensuing battle, the Battle of Eutaw Springs, was a bitterly contested and bloody affair, and would turn out to be the last major engagement of the Revolutionary War in South Carolina. Greene wrote to Rutledge at Mount Joseph the day after the battle: "We have a most Obstinate and Bloody action — Victory was ours."[29]

During that day, a continuous line of British prisoners passed by Mount Joseph, to be shuttled in small groups across the Congaree at McCord's Ferry. John Rutledge interviewed some of the prisoners to gather as much information about the battle as he could to send to the South Carolina delegates in Philadelphia. "Two hundred and sixty prisoners made the crossing," he wrote, "the rest so badly wounded they must come on more slowly."[30] The badly wounded prisoners probably stayed for a while at Mount Joseph where Rebecca and the others would have tried their best to alleviate their sufferings.

While Greene was writing "Victory is ours" to Rutledge, Colonel Stewart was also claiming victory, though his losses had been very heavy. If Eutaw Springs was a British victory, it was a hollow one. Soon after the battle, the British abandoned their position. Greene had achieved his objective: he had driven the British from the territory they had possessed, and although they had not been driven completely out of the southeast, they were confined to the coast. After controlling all of Georgia and South Carolina, the British now held only Savannah and Charleston. As distressing as this situation was, there was an even more distressing situation developing for them in Virginia.

While British and American forces were clashing at Eutaw Springs, Lord Cornwallis was in Virginia occupying Yorktown — a port located on the York River at the point where the river empties into the Chesapeake Bay. Unfortunately, at the end of September, Cornwallis found himself trapped there with the French fleet blocking the entrance to the bay and the combined armies of General Washington and the Comte de Rochambeau blocking the land approaches. The Siege of Yorktown began on September 29 and ended with the British surrender on October 19. In the course of only two months, the British war effort had suffered two devasting blows — a substantial loss of territory in South Carolina and Georgia and the loss of an entire army at Yorktown.

The victory at Yorktown was hailed with great joy by Patriots in all the colonies, and no one would have celebrated it with more pleasure than Rebecca. A spirit of optimism spread among Patriots, and now that the British had been driven out of Georgetown and were confined, for the most part, to Charleston, Rebecca would have felt the time was right for her to return to Fairfield. However, although the war was winding down, Tory militia were still active in parts of South Carolina, especially in the Orangeburg area where Tories from Ninety Six had relocated. It would not be safe for a group of women and children to make the journey from Mount Joseph to Fairfield without an armed escort. General Greene had once more retired to the High Hills of Santee to rest his troops, and Rebecca asked for his help. On November 9, 1781, Captain Nathaniel Pendleton, one of Greene's aides, issued an order to Lt. James Simmons to take six dragoons and escort Rebecca Motte from her Congaree home to her plantation on the Santee.[31]

Chapter Ten

The British Evacuation of South Carolina

When Rebecca and her daughters reached Fairfield in the middle of November, the handsome mansion house was still standing on the bluff overlooking the river with the rice fields stretching off into the distance. As the familiar scene burst into view, Rebecca must have wondered how many of her enslaved workers she would find still on the property, and in what condition she would find the house. It would not have mattered; Fairfield was home. She had spent much of the twenty-three years of her married life there, and after the turmoil and sorrow of the past year-and-a-half, it would have appeared to her as a kind of haven, no matter its condition. Perhaps amid its familiar surroundings she would be able to find solace and a modicum of tranquility. Her return certainly began well. Good news arrived from Philadelphia. In October, Betsey had given birth to a baby girl, Elizabeth Brewton Pinckney, and both mother and daughter were reported to be doing well.

Meanwhile, the war continued to wind down. In November, while Rebecca and her daughters were settling in at Fairfield, General Leslie arrived in Charleston to take over as the commander of the British army. Leslie immediately began to consolidate his troops. On November 18, the British post at Wilmington, North Carolina was evacuated, and the soldiers there — along with a large number of Loyalists and their enslaved servants — were brought to Charleston. In South Carolina, Leslie drew all his troops into town, establishing outposts at Monck's Corner and Dorchester. The British army was now confined to an area that lay within a 20-mile radius of Charleston.

General Greene had succeeded in his mission and it was now time for Governor Rutledge to carry out his plan to establish civil government in the state. Before he could call for elections to be held, however, Rutledge needed to designate the place where the legislature was to meet. He decided on the little town of Jacksonborough, located thirty-six miles west of Charleston.

Once the location for the meeting had been chosen, Greene moved his headquarters from the High Hills of Santee to Bacon's Bridge on the Ashely River, twenty-four miles from town. From this position he could make sure the British remained confined to the area around Charleston and, since Jacksonborough was only 20 miles away, he could offer protection to the members of the legislature, should the British try to disrupt the meetings. Rutledge then called for elections to take place for the first meeting of the General Assembly to be held in South Carolina in two years.

As the year 1781 wound to a close, those who supported the American cause had reason to be optimistic and proud of what had been accomplished. The British had been confined to the coast, elections had been held, and the legislature was scheduled to meet in January at the beginning of the new year. Yet, in spite of these accomplishments, Patriots understood they needed to remain vigilant — the war was not over, and clashes between British and American forces were still taking place. This was especially true in the Georgetown and Santee areas which were rapidly becoming areas of importance to both sides.

The Santee area with its rice fields and well-stocked plantations most attracted the interest of the British. They were struggling to feed the thousands of Loyalist refugees and their enslaved servants who had poured into Charleston with the retreating troops and looked to this rich agricultural area to supplement their dwindling food supplies. Foraging parties routinely rode out from town to commandeer rice, hogs, cattle, and fodder from plantations between Charleston and the Santee River. Unfortunately for Rebecca, Fairfield lay in this area, and she was once again faced with the possibility of receiving unexpected visits from the enemy.

While the territory south of the Santee River had become important to the British, that to the north had become essential to the Americans. Unlike his British counterpart, Greene not only needed food for his army, but also everything from arms and ammunition, to shoes, shirts, blankets, and saddles. In the past the army's supplies had come overland from Philadelphia to Camden by way of the Great Wagon Road. But now that the British had abandoned Georgetown, the town had become the port of entry for supplies and communications coming from the north.

The region around Georgetown was also important, for it was a prime area for the production of salt — an essential commodity for the army. Although the British had been dislodged from Georgetown, they still commanded the sea, and could attack Georgetown, raid the countryside, or capture ships laden with supplies. Francis Marion, who was operating south of the Santee, sent Peter Horry, his second-in-command, to protect the northern region.

As the new year began, Rebecca received some exciting news from Philadelphia. Tom and Betsey were anxious to come home and were growing tired of waiting for Tom's exchange to be arranged so they could leave. Having heard that the British were abandoning their outlying posts and retreating towards Charleston, Tom felt he could safely return to Santee and wait there for his exchange. Betsey was recovering from childbirth, and she and the baby would be strong enough to travel by the end of January. Rebecca was informed the family was planning to leave Philadelphia at that time and journey south by carriage. It would have certainly been very welcome news — both for the family at Fairfield, and for Tom's mother and sister at Hampton.

Meanwhile, Rebecca was helping the Patriot cause by suppling provisions and other goods to the army — a practice started by her husband in the early years of the war, and one she had continued after his death. Indeed, records show that after the war, Rebecca was paid for providing "sundries for Continentals and Militia" from 1778 to 1783.[1] The word "sundries" indicates that it was not only food that she and Jacob provided, but also other goods such as boats, carts, wagons, and the labor of enslaved workers.

In January, a shoe factory was started in the Georgetown area to provide Greene's army with much-needed footwear. The superintendent had permission to impress enslaved workers from the area to work in the factory. At the beginning of March, more enslaved workers were needed to build up defenses around Georgetown in expectation of a British attack. It is highly likely that Rebecca supplied enslaved labor from her plantation for one, if not both of these endeavors.

In the middle of March, Tom, Betsey, and the children arrived safely at Fairfield, no doubt exhausted after the long, tedious journey, but delighted to be home at last. Rebecca would have been excited to see them both, and to have a chance to dote on her grandchildren. Little Tom, whom she had not seen since he was a baby, was now eighteen months old, walking and probably beginning to utter a few recognizable words. Then there was baby Elizabeth, five months old, just waiting to be admired and fussed over by her grandmother and her two fond aunts.

In addition to Betsey, her husband, and the two children, there was another guest staying at Fairfield in March. His name was Henry Pendleton. Originally from Virginia, Henry was the nephew of Edmund Pendleton, a well-known Virginia planter, lawyer, and politician. Henry, like his uncle, was a lawyer, and in 1776 had become a state judge in South Carolina. Captain Nathaniel Pendleton, the aide to General Greene who had ordered the dragoons to escort Rebecca to Fairfield, was his brother.

American Patriot and Successful Rice Planter

Henry, an ardent Patriot, had remained in Charleston during the siege, and in his capacity as a judge, had ordered three Tories to be hanged just a few days before the city fell. It was a courageous act, but one that put him in great danger of losing his own life when the British took command of the city. Fortunately, although he had surrendered with the other civilians in town, he managed to escape and make his way to Philadelphia where his story made the rounds and he became something of a celebrity.[2]

At the beginning of the year, Henry decided, just as Thomas Pinckney had done, that it was safe to return to South Carolina and had made his way south, accepting an invitation to stay at Fairfield. How this invitation happened to be extended is not known. It is possible that Rebecca was already acquainted with Henry, and upon hearing he was coming to the area, invited him to stay at her house. However, even if Rebecca had not known him personally, she would have certainly known who Henry was and what he had done, and would not have hesitated to offer hospitality to a courageous Patriot who had defied the British. Regrettably, her invitation had unpleasant consequences for them both.

It happened on the morning of Wednesday, March 27. Betsey and Tom, accompanied by one of Betsey's sisters, had gone to pay a call at nearby Hampton plantation, while Rebecca, her other daughter, and Henry Pendleton remained at Fairfield. Tom's sister and brother-in-law were not at home, having been detained in Charleston. But Eliza Pinckney, Tom's mother, and little Harriott Horry, his niece, were at the house.[3] Also staying at Hampton was Major Hyrne, a former aide-de-camp to General Greene. As he was reported to be "in a bad State of Health," Hyrne may have been staying at Hampton to recover from an illness.[4]

Secrets were difficult to keep in the countryside as people, both free and enslaved, were constantly traveling between plantations, and news and gossip tended to spread quickly. It would not have taken long for Loyalists in the area to hear that there were prominent Patriots staying at Fairfield and Hampton. Always on the alert for useful information to pass on to the British, the Tories would have taken great delight in disclosing to them that the "infamous" Judge Pendleton could be found at Fairfield, and a former aide-de-camp to General Greene at Hampton. On the morning of Wednesday, March 27, a British patrol under the command of Major Fraser set out for Santee to take the rebels into custody.

That morning, as Rebecca was going about her daily activities, she received word that a party of British dragoons was headed to Fairfield. She would have instantly realized she needed to hide her guest before the dragoons reached the house. But where? It had to be someplace that was not obvious. It is not known who came up with the idea — Rebecca, her daughter, Henry or one of the enslaved servants — but it was soon decided that the best place to hide Henry was in a rug. He was most likely whisked up to the garret and quickly and carefully rolled up inside one of the carpets being stored there.[5]

Meanwhile, Major Fraser had divided his patrol into two groups, sending one to Fairfield to apprehend Judge Pendleton, while he took the other half to Hampton in search of Major Hyrne. The party of dragoons sent to Fairfield, encountering only two women and without the controlling presence of Major Fraser, their commanding officer decided to take advantage of the situation. According to Tom Pinckney in his report to General Greene, Mrs. Motte and her daughter "were much insulted and plundered" by the British party who came there.[6] Indeed, it would have been a frightening experience for Rebecca and her daughter to be pushed aside while armed men rummaged through their home, no doubt turning everything upside down and pocketing any object that took their fancy.

When the search of the house proved fruitless, the two women must have breathed a great sigh of relief. However, any hope Rebecca might have cherished that the dragoons would now leave was soon dashed. Not finding their quarry on their first search of the house, the British searched three more times, finding Rebecca's unfortunate guest on the fourth attempt and taking him away.[7]

While the British were ransacking the house at Fairfield, Major Fraser and the other half of the patrol were descending on Hampton plantation, where they found two people of interest — Major Hyrne and Major Thomas Pinckney. The dragoons immediately took Hyrne into custody and would have taken Tom also, until he explained he was a prisoner-on-parole waiting to be exchanged or, he would have added, if he had been exchanged, he had gotten no official word of it. Fraser finally agreed to allow Tom to remain at liberty, but only on the condition that he give himself up if they found, upon their return to town, that his exchange had already taken place — a promise Tom was happy to make.

In contrast to the behavior of the soldiers at Fairfield, Tom reported to General Greene that Fraser and the other officers who came to Hampton had "behaved with Politeness" during the entire encounter — Fraser even going to the extent of condemning the looting that had taken place at Fairfield. When he saw the party that had gone to Fairfield arrive at Hampton with their prisoner and their saddlebags full of stolen goods, Fraser, according to Tom, "made the Dragoons deliver up part of their Plunder & promised to procure the rest when more at leisure."[8] Whether this promise was ever kept is not known, but at least some of Rebecca's possessions would have been returned to her.

At this point, Fraser and his men would have returned to Charleston with their captives, then turned them over to the British authorities in town. Judge Pendleton and Major Hyrne were likely kept in close confinement until they were either exchanged for British prisoners held by the Americans or until the general exchange of all prisoners-of-war was arranged.

Although Loyalists may have wanted to see Judge Pendleton executed for hanging the three Tories before the surrender of Charleston, the war was coming to a close and General Leslie, the British commander, was too politically astute to risk the recriminations that would occur if he were to order Pendleton to be hanged.

After the British left with their prisoners, the family at Fairfield would spend several anxious days waiting for a response to Tom's letter to General Greene requesting confirmation of his status: was he still a prisoner-on-parole or had his exchange taken place? Fortunately, the news, when it arrived, was good — he was still a prisoner-on-parole and, therefore, did not have to turn himself in to the British.

But Tom would have been anxious not to encounter another British patrol, for even though he was still a prisoner-on-parole, he was supposed to be in Philadelphia awaiting his exchange, not in South Carolina. He could not be sure the next British commander he met would be as accommodating as Major Fraser had been. Consequently, since the enemy's cavalry seemed disposed to visit the area south of the Santee, he decided to move. He "borrowed" an unoccupied house located on the north side of the river where he hoped not to be bothered by the enemy.[9]

While Rebecca and her family had been busily engaged at Fairfield during the first few months of the year, the General Assembly had met in Jacksonborough. The legislators had a full agenda. They began by electing John Matthews as the new governor and then settled down to consider the passage of a number of bills. One bill, in particular, took up a great deal of their time. It was an important bill and one that would affect the lives of many South Carolinians — including people close to Rebecca.

American Patriot and Successful Rice Planter

Patriots in South Carolina had suffered greatly during the British occupation of their state. They had seen their houses and fields burned, their animals slaughtered, their crops destroyed, and wagons, boats, horses, and enslaved workers commandeered by the enemy. Some had their property seized outright by the British, and hundreds of Patriots — men, women, and children — had been sent into exile. That meant the delegates who filed into the General Assembly meeting on January 18, 1782, were in a vindictive mood — anxious to seek revenge on those who had supported the British cause. The result was the introduction of a piece of legislation that would allow the state to confiscate the property of Loyalists and to either confiscate or amerce (fine) the estates of those who had been Patriots but then taken British protection. Known as the Confiscation Act, the bill had widespread support and passed with little opposition.

While the passage of the Confiscation Act had been relatively simple, determining the list of people whose property was to be confiscated or amerced was more difficult. Ned Rutledge, the author of the first draft of the bill, wrote to his brother-in-law Arthur Middleton in Philadelphia on February 8: "I do assure you my dear Friend the passions of some People run very high. Tho' I am for Confiscating some Estates yet I fear some men will give way to private Resentment — it is an odious painful Business."[10] Ned Rutledge was quite correct. Personal feelings did play a prominent role in the selection of names to be placed on the list, and many men fell victim to the vindictiveness of their peers. One of these men was Charles Pinckney, II, the husband of Frances Brewton Pinckney — Rebecca's sister.

Charles had been a strong Patriot supporter at the beginning of the war, donating 20,000 guineas (a gold coin worth a little over a pound) to the war effort. He had also been a member of the new, independent government of South Carolina — serving in the upper house of the legislature and later becoming a member of the governor's council. In fact, he had been one of the three council members who accompanied Governor Rutledge to Georgetown a month before the fall of Charleston. However, after the surrender of the town, when Governor Rutledge was about to leave the state to take refuge in North Carolina, Pinckney could not bring himself to accompany him.

While Pinckney had been in Georgetown with the governor, his wife and four youngest children had been at Snee Farm Plantation, the Pinckney country estate located ten miles north of Charleston. During the weeks leading up to the surrender, the British conducted numerous raids on plantations in the area, and Snee Farm, the home of a prominent member of the rebel government, had been a prime target. The enemy, it was reported, had carried away all the silverware, linen, and provisions at the plantation, leaving Frances and the children virtually helpless. Pinckney, fearing his family would be left to starve if he accompanied the governor to North Carolina, returned to Charleston and surrendered to the British.

Unfortunately, Pinckney had made political enemies during his long career in government and they now joined to denounce him in the General Assembly. There were two serious charges leveled against him. The first was that he had voluntarily returned to Charleston and taken British protection when he could have remained at liberty with the governor. The second was that he was one of the approximately 160 Charlestonians who had signed a letter congratulating Cornwallis on his victory at Camden and denouncing the struggle for independence. Although John Sandford Dart, one of his supporters in the legislature, spoke in his defense, his main political adversary, Christopher Gadsden, was more persuasive, and Pinckney's estate was amerced twelve percent of its net worth.

News of the passage of the Confiscation Act spread quickly throughout the state, causing a great deal of consternation among the Loyalists in Charleston. It took longer for the names of those who were to have their property confiscated or amerced to be known, as the legislature debated long and hard over who was to be included. When the list of names was complete, the delegates issued an ultimatum: all former Patriots living under British protection in Charleston had until August, when the next meeting of the General Assembly was scheduled, to leave town and report to American headquarters at Bacon's Bridge. Those who did not "come out" faced confiscation of property and banishment from the state.

Rebecca would have been aghast at the news that her brother-in-law's estate was to be amerced, but she would have confidently expected to hear very soon that he had "come out" and reported to the authorities at American headquarters. However, Pinckney, ashamed of his actions and humiliated by the criticism he had received from the members of the General Assembly, flinched from the prospect of coming out of town and facing his peers. Therefore, when weeks passed with no word that he had "come out," Rebecca was very anxious to get in touch with her sister.

But communicating with someone in British-held Charleston was no easy matter as Charles Cotesworth Pinckney discovered when he tried to send a letter to his cousin, Charles Pinckney. Charles Cotesworth, having received his exchange, had returned to South Carolina in April, and reported to General Greene at American headquarters. Surprised to find his cousin's name on the list of people whose property was to be amerced, he was further shocked when he discovered his cousin was making no effort to "come out." Not wanting to see a man he had always admired stripped of his property and banished from the land of his birth, he wrote Charles a letter encouraging him to leave British protection. He thought he had found a person willing to take the letter through British lines into town, but, unfortunately, at the last minute the gentleman decided it was too risky and so returned the letter.[11]

Rebecca faced a similar dilemma in trying to correspond with her sister. All civilians who wanted to travel into Charleston, or to send their enslaved servants into town, had to have an authorized pass. In fact, the governor had decreed that women who went into town without a pass were not to be allowed to return, while slaves who carried provisions or intelligence to the enemy were to be executed. Francis Marion had been put in charge of issuing the passes in the Santee area.

The phrase: "it is better to ask forgiveness than permission" was probably not used in the 18th century, but most people at that time would have understood the basic concept behind the statement. Apparently, Rebecca understood it, for instead of applying for a pass, which would have certainly been denied, she began to routinely send a boat into Charleston with a few of her enslaved servants onboard, most likely with letters to Frances hidden in their clothing, or verbal messages to her carried in their heads. The enslaved servants would have then carried messages from Frances back to Rebecca.

How long she was able to correspond with her sister in this manner is not known, but her activities had not gone unnoticed. On May 24, Francis Marion wrote to Peter Horry, ordering him to seize Mrs. Motte's boat and slaves "and make prize of them, agreeable to the Governor's proclamation.... She has no pass from the Governor, Gen. Greene, or myself, nor no other person; they wish a stop put to it."[12]

The loss of her contact with Charleston was a double loss for Rebecca, for she not only lost her means of communicating with her sister, but she also lost her main source of information about the Horrys. Daniel Horry, who had taken British protection after the fall of Charleston, had gone to England in the summer of 1781 to enroll his son in school. On his return to Charleston in late February, Daniel had been shocked to find his name on the list of people whose property was to be confiscated. To make matters worse, the British refused to allow him to leave Charleston.

Harriott had applied for and been given permission to join him in town in the middle of March. As a result, unease over the fate of her good friend and her family was added to Rebecca's worry about her sister and her family.

As the summer progressed, however, news began to trickle out from the American headquarters at Bacon's Bridge. Some of it was encouraging. Daniel Horry's property was not to be confiscated, only amerced, and the amercement was postponed as he was appealing the decision. Then in August, Rebecca heard that Charles Pinckney had finally "come out" and reported to American headquarters — which was a great relief to her.

The next report from American headquarters, however, would have caused Rebecca some concern: Charles Pinckney was reported to be seriously ill. He had been under a great deal of stress during the months leading up to his journey to Bacon's Bridge, and as a result, was in a weakened condition when he arrived at the American Headquarters in August. Unfortunately, there in the countryside away from Charleston and its sea breezes, he contracted malaria and did not have the strength to resist it. He died on September 22, 1782. His body could not be brought into British-held Charleston for burial so he was temporarily laid to rest in the graveyard at St. Andrew's Church on the Ashley River.[13] The fact that Rebecca could not be with her sister and nieces and nephews at this difficult time must have weighted heavily on her mind.

In spite of her worries, Rebecca's spirits would have been somewhat lifted by the encouraging rumors that were circulating throughout the countryside that fall. It was said that the war might soon be over. The rumors were well-founded. Weary of the long, expensive war, the combatants had sent representatives to Paris in April to begin peace negotiations. In America the British had evacuated Savannah in July, and on August 7 General Leslie officially announced his intention of withdrawing from Charleston.

Meanwhile, Greene remained encamped on the west side of the Ashley River, keeping a watchful eye on British activities and waiting for a sign that the evacuation was about to begin. The sign finally came in December, when a sizable fleet of British ships began to arrive in Charleston harbor. Greene then ordered Brigadier General Anthony Wayne with 300 light infantry troops, 80 members of Lee's cavalry, and 20 artillery men with two six-pounders to cross the Ashley River and take up a position near the British fortifications north of Charleston. Once they reached their destination, Wayne and his men encamped and settled down to wait.

While the Americans were waiting north of town, General Leslie was in town busily overseeing the evacuation of 14,000 people — crown officials, British, Hessian, and provincial troops, civilian refugees, and over 5,000 people of African descent who had been enslaved but were now free. It had taken two days for this large mass of people to board the 130 ships riding at anchor in the harbor, and there was now only one group left to embark — the soldiers guarding the fortifications north of town.[14]

On December 13, Leslie sent a message to General Wayne, informing him that he was planning to leave the city the next day. Leslie added that if "no impediment should be offered" to the embarkation of the remaining British troops, "he pledged himself that no injury should be done to the town." However, he continued, in the event of an attack, he would not be "answerable to any consequences that may follow."[15] General Wayne agreed. The Americans would not hinder or interrupt the British withdrawal in any way, and in return, the British would not harm the town.

At daybreak on Saturday, December 14, the morning gun was fired, the sound echoing over the sleeping city. It was a signal to the British troops manning the fortifications outside the city's northern gates that it was time to leave. When the British soldiers began their march toward town, the Americans followed at a discreet distance. Then, as the British passed through the city gates and veered off toward Gadsden's Wharf to board one of the military transports anchored in the harbor, the Americans proceeded into town.

Wayne and his men moved cautiously through the silent and empty streets of the city. The inhabitants of Charleston — British merchants who had received permission to stay to collect debts and sell their wares, Loyalists who elected to take their chances with the Patriots rather than leave their homeland, and Patriots who had had no recourse but to remain in town during the siege and subsequent occupation — had all been warned by the British to stay inside until the transfer had been complete. British warships were in the harbor and the Royal Navy was standing by to repel any last-minute attack should the Americans decide to launch one.[16] However, all remained quiet, and by eleven o'clock the American forces were at the statehouse. After being occupied by the British for two years, seven months and two days, Charleston was once again in the possession of the Americans.

Chapter Eleven
The End of the War and a New Beginning

It took the British fleet three days to depart. It was not until the 17th of December that the last ship crossed the bar and sailed out into the Atlantic. At that time, the Americans, who had politely refrained from raising their standard while the British ships were in the harbor, hoisted the American flag to fly proudly over the city.[1] The British were truly gone, and Charlestonians could now safely return to their homes.

It was probably at this time that Rebecca returned to Charleston. Knowing that both General Clinton and Colonel Balfour had used the Miles Brewton house as their headquarters, she would have been wondering in what condition she would find it. Upon her arrival, she probably found the gardens had been neglected and the house showed some signs of wear and tear, as the previous occupants would have had little interest in seeing that it was properly maintained. There was something curious in the south parlor, though. Etched into the beautiful marble mantel over the fireplace was a collection of drawings: two 18th-Century square-rigged warships, three other vessels, and a profile caricature of a man with "Sir H. Clinton" carved underneath.[2]

How pleased Rebecca must have been to be back in town and close to her sister once again. They had not seen each other since the spring of 1780, when the British began their siege, and the intervening two-and-a-half years had been filled with sorrow and stress for both of them. There must have been many times during that period when they longed for one another's company. Now they could visit as often as they liked.

American Patriot and Successful Rice Planter

In addition to her sister, Rebecca would have been anxious to see other family members and acquaintances , and no doubt, as soon as they were settled in, she and her daughters were out paying calls and receiving visitors at their home. It would have been an exciting time for the three of them as they reconnected with their relatives and friends and caught up on the latest news. One of the many visitors Rebecca and her daughters would welcome to the house on King Street was a young officer from Lee's Legion whom they had met during the Siege of Fort Motte. His name was John Middleton, and he was likely given a very warm reception.

Although born and educated in England, John had a South Carolina connection — his father, William Middleton, had been born in South Carolina and was the older brother of Henry Middleton. Although William had left the colony in 1754 to live on his estates in England, he had always remained greatly attached to the land of his birth and had sided with the colonies in their disputes with the mother country. John, apparently influenced by his father's support for the American cause, came to America early in the war to offer his services in the fight for independence. In 1779, he had become a member of Lee's Legion.

Now, having resigned his commission in the Legion, John, it appears, was planning to make his home in South Carolina and was anxious to renew his acquaintance with Rebecca and her daughters — especially Fanny. The attraction between John and Fanny, which had most likely begun during the Siege of Fort Motte, turned into a serious courtship in the weeks that followed, and the young couple was soon making plans to be married. Rebecca would have been very pleased to welcome John into the family — a well-connected young man who had come all the way from England to fight for American independence could not have failed to find favor with her.

The citizens of Charleston, happy to be back in town and rid of the British, could not rest easy just yet, however. The British no longer had a presence in South Carolina, but they still occupied New York City and the war was not officially over. General Greene had not disbanded the army in case hostilities broke out again, and in Charleston, the governor and the legislature faced a myriad of problems. A feeling of uncertainty hung in the air. Nevertheless, the courts were functioning once again, and Rebecca had a legal obligation to fulfill. Jacob Motte had died without making a will, and it was time to begin the process of settling his estate.

On February 10, 1783, Rebecca appeared in court, where she was granted the power to administer her husband's estate: to collect all monies owed to him and to pay his debts as far as his estate would allow. She was also given three months to make an inventory of all his property.[3] Making the inventory was a relatively simple process, but ascertaining the amount of money owed to Jacob Motte and the extent of his debts, collecting the former and paying the latter, was another matter entirely.

South Carolina was facing an economic crisis. For eight years Carolinians had been limited in their ability to sell their crops abroad, and as a result had been living on credit — accumulating large amounts of debt. These debts were now due, and planters and farmers alike lacked the means to pay them. The war had left the countryside in shambles, and many plantations and farms were ruined or nearly ruined. Therefore, instead of planting crops to repay their debts, many in the state were faced with the prospect of having to sink even deeper into debt by borrowing money to repair damages to their property and to purchase enslaved workers to replace those carried off by the British.

The situation was made even more difficult by the lack of money in the state. The paper money issued by the government during the war had depreciated to the point that few creditors were willing to accept it. Gold and silver coins were in short supply as Eliza Lucas Pinckney explained to a friend in England

American Patriot and Successful Rice Planter

for whom she was trying to collect a debt. "I do not believe that all that are indebted to you tho' people of property could at this time command 50 Guinea's so scarce is gold and silver and such is the deplorable state of our Country."[4]

Needless to say, these were chaotic times. As the contemporary historian David Ramsay later wrote, "Eight years of war in Carolina were followed by eight years of disorganization which produced such an amount of civil distress as diminished with some their respect for liberty and independence."[5] It was in this unfavorable environment that Rebecca struggled to administer her husband's estate and forge a new life for herself and her teen-aged daughter.

Yet there were some bright spots during the year 1783. Fanny and John were married on July 31, and at the end of the year, Fanny announced that she was expecting a child. On September 3, the Treaty of Paris was signed, officially ending the war. The United States of America was now recognized by the European powers as an independent country. Unfortunately, the official end of the war only added to the problems facing South Carolinians. Under the terms of the Treaty of Paris, the United States was prohibited from trading with the British colonies in the West Indies, cutting off a major market for Carolina produce and a prime source of gold and silver coins.

Still, the settlement of Jacob's estate proceeded on schedule. On January 6, 1784, Thomas Pinckney and John Middleton, representing their wives, who as married women had no legal status, and Rebecca as the guardian of the 15-year-old Mary, petitioned the court of common pleas for a Writ of Partition to divide Jacob's property equally among his children. The court-appointed five commissioners to make the division, and by March 25, they were ready to issue their report.

The commissioners had not been able to divide Jacob's property equally, as Fairfield, which had been given to Betsey, was more valuable than the property allotted to her sisters. Therefore, Betsey and Tom were ordered to pay Fanny and Mary £500 sterling each to compensate for the difference in the value of their inheritances. In addition to the £500, Fanny received 500 acres of land on the Savannah River, 452 acres of land on Cedar Island located at the mouth of the Santee River, 600 acres at Red Bank on the Cooper River, and several town-lots in Beaufort, Georgetown and Charleston. Mary was given 550 acres of land on the Congaree River, several large town-lots in Amelia Township, plus the £500 from Betsey and Tom.[6]

As a widow, Rebecca was entitled to her dower right — usually one-third of the husband's estate. However, when Jacob and Rebecca were married, Jacob Motte Sr. had placed Motte's Wharf in trust for his son, his son's wife, and their children. Therefore, Motte's Wharf with the rental income from the warehouses, stores, and other buildings located there constituted Rebecca's dower.[7] She, of course, still owned Mount Joseph plantation and half the house on King Street. Rebecca and her sister were also co-owners of other properties that had belonged to Miles Brewton, but it is not known how many of these properties were still in their possession at this time.

The extent of the debts owed by Jacob Motte is not known. He had been a merchant, and in extending credit to many of his customers in the past, had put himself in debt to his suppliers abroad. As a merchant-banker, Jacob had also made loans to his fellow South Carolinians. For example, records indicate that on July 25, 1776, Jacob lent William Garner £6,000 in South Carolina currency, with Garner's promise to repay £3,000 of the loan plus eight percent interest in July of 1777. Yet the entire loan was still outstanding at the end of the war. Moreover, William Garner was probably not the only person who had borrowed money from Jacob Motte and not repaid it.[8]

The good news for Rebecca was that Jacob's creditors could not touch Motte's Wharf, as it was held in trust for her and her children, nor the property she inherited from her brother. However, they could seize Jacob's estate, endangering the property her daughters had just inherited — a course of action that Rebecca would have found unacceptable. Jacob's debts had to be paid. Fortunately, the legislature stepped in at this point to give Rebecca and other debtors some breathing room.

In 1784, the General Assembly passed an act prohibiting creditors from suing for debts contracted in the past until the year 1786. At this time, they would be allowed to sue annually for one-quarter (later changed to one-fifth) of the amount owed.[9] Although this act gave Rebecca some relief in settling with Jacob's creditors, it also postponed her ability to collect debts owed to her husband.

The next year the Sheriff's Sale Act of 1785 was passed, authorizing the use of land as legal tender for the payment of debts. Many creditors faced with the choice of having to accept land of questionable value in remote areas of the state or extending the time of repayment chose the latter course. In 1787 this act was replaced by the Installment Act, which allowed debtors to repay debts in installments with the final payment not due until 1790.

It is likely that during this time Rebecca came to a satisfactory arrangement with Jacob's major creditors. She may have even pledged her own holdings as security, promising to sell them as soon as the time was right — the overabundance of land on the market making this an inauspicious time to sell property. Jacob's creditors would have been very happy to accept this arrangement, as they would have infinitely preferred to be paid in the future with cash instead of being paid now with land.

Rebecca planned to sell Mount Joseph plantation and, with her daughters' permission, Motte's Wharf as soon as it was feasible.[10] In the next few years, she and her sister Frances, who was struggling to pay the amercement levied by the government on her husband's estate, also sold the Miles Brewton House, a lot on Tradd Street left to them by their brother,[11] and whatever property they had inherited that had not already been sold. Since Rebecca could not be sure that the sale of these properties would net enough to meet the demands of all Jacob's creditors, she would need to have another source of revenue to pay what might remain and support herself.

Rebecca made a bold decision — she became a rice planter. Rice was the most valuable commodity produced in South Carolina at this time, and she had experience in its production. For twenty-three years, she had helped Jacob manage Fairfield and had managed it by herself for three years after his death. It was a familiar and comfortable occupation for her. The fact that she had no money to buy a plantation or the enslaved labor needed to work it did not seem to deter her, and with her customary determination she set out to achieve her goal.

Fortunately, in February of 1784 the executors of the last will and testament of Sampson Neyle were ready to auction off his Santee lands. Neyle, a neighbor and friend of the Motte's in Santee, and the owner of several rice plantations in the area, had died in June 1780, leaving no heirs, having lost his only son during the Siege of Charleston and his wife shortly after. This was prime rice-producing land, and John Middleton, anxious to establish himself as a rice planter, bought Washo plantation from Neyle's estate. Located between Washo and Fairfield were two small plantations containing two hundred acres each — a perfect situation for Rebecca. She persuaded the executors of the estate to accept her bond for £3,400 plus interest for the property and all the "appurtenances" belonging to the land. On July 12, 1784, the papers were signed, and Rebecca found herself the proud owner of a rice plantation.[12]

Buying the land was the first step. Now she needed to acquire labor — for without labor, the land was virtually worthless. There does not appear to be any record of where Rebecca obtained the enslaved workers she needed for her plantation. It is possible that the executors of Samson Neyle's estate were also auctioning off his enslaved labor force in addition to his land, and that Rebecca purchased her workers from Neyle's estate. However, wherever she acquired them, she had to have purchased them on credit, adding to the amount of debt she was accumulating.

Rebecca decided to call her plantation Eldorado, for the golden flowers she found growing there in such great profusion. Although there were probably buildings on the property, most likely there was no owner's house, for Rebecca continued to live at Fairfield for several more years, managing her property from there.[13]

That summer, to Rebecca's great delight, Fanny gave birth to a baby boy — John Middleton Jr. It is possible that the birth of a son prompted Middleton to buy Crowfield, the Goose Creek plantation that had once belonged to his father. William Middleton had sold the plantation in 1754 when he went to live in England, and after changing hands several times, the property was purchased by Rawlins Lowndes in 1776. He was now willing to sell it to John.[14]

Sometime in the fall of 1784, the deal was complete, and Crowfield was once again in the hands of the Middleton family. Unfortunately, a few weeks after the purchase, John fell ill. He had a high fever and his skin turned yellow. No doubt Rebecca hurried to Washo to help Fanny care for her husband, but their efforts, combined with those of the doctor, were to no avail. On November 14, 1784, John Middleton died.

Rebecca must have been heartbroken for her daughter. Fanny, at the age of twenty-one, was a widow with a small baby and the two rice plantations her husband had recently purchased to manage, plus all the property she had inherited from her father.

It is quite possible that at this sad time in her life, Fanny and her baby stayed at Fairfield where both Rebecca and Tom Pinckney were available to give her advice on the management of her affairs.

On June 6, 1785, Rebecca placed the following melancholy notice in the newspaper: "For Public Sale on Monday the 18th of July at the home of Mrs. Rebecca Motte in King Street…Several articles of neat Furniture, entirely new, belonging to the estate of John Middleton, Esq., deceased." Among the articles offered for sale were several looking glasses with carved and burnished gold frames, mahogany bedsteads, complete with bed curtains, pillows, mattresses, etc., a new, London-made phaeton (a light, open, four-wheeled, horse-drawn carriage), a second-hand phaeton made in Philadelphia and three valuable saddle horses.[15] In effect, Fanny was selling the things she and John had purchased to start their new life together — most of which had, undoubtedly, been bought on credit.

Ironically, one year almost to the day after Rebecca had attended John Middleton's sickbed, she was called on to attend another. Daniel Horry was ill at Hampton with a "bilious fever." When Rebecca arrived at Hampton and saw Daniel, her heart must have sunk — his skin was "as yellow as the darkest Orange," very much like John Middleton's had been, and she would have feared the worst.[16] Harriott sent for a doctor from Charleston, but there was little he could do, and on November 12, 1785, Horry died.

Rebecca, her daughter Fanny, and her closest friend Harriott were now all widows facing the challenge of navigating the masculine world of rice production in the chaotic environment of post-war South Carolina. They were all three in debt. Rebecca owed money on the property she had bought, and records indicate that John Middleton had given several bonds, one for

£1,200 to Lowndes, presumably for the purchase of Crowfield,[17] and he may have even owed money on the Washo plantation, while Harriott had the amercement levied by the government on her husband's estate to pay. They would need to band together, share information and ideas, and support each other if they were to be successful. They were soon joined by another widow with considerable experience in the masculine world of agriculture — Eliza Lucas Pinckney. Harriott had asked her sixty-three-year-old mother to come live with her at Hampton after Daniel's death. No doubt she was more than willing to lend moral support to the three women rice planters.

Like most agricultural pursuits, rice planting was completely dependent on the weather. If there was too little rain early in the planting season, the plants would not fully develop, while too much rain later on, or rain at the wrong time, could disrupt the harvesting of the grain or cause the unthreshed rice to mold or decay. Just as Rebecca and other rice planters were hoping for a good crop in 1784 and 1785 to help ease their financial situations, the weather did not cooperate. During those two years, the situation was so dire that the average amount of rice exported from South Carolina amounted to less than 50,000 barrels a year, while ten years earlier the average had been 129,000 barrels.[18]

The agricultural situation in the state clearly called for some kind of action. On August 9, 1785, a group of concerned planters — all male — met and formed the South Carolina Society for Promoting and Improving Agriculture and other Rural Concerns. Thomas Heyward Jr. and Thomas Pinckney were elected president and vice-president respectively. The society's goal was to improve agricultural methods and animal breeding and to encourage the diversification of crops so that the state would have more products to offer and could seek new markets.

While Rebecca, Fanny, and Harriott, as unmarried women, were able to conduct business — borrow money, buy and sell property, sue in court, etc. — they could not be members of the Society for Promoting and Improving Agriculture, and would not have been privy to information about the latest agricultural innovations. They were not at all concerned, however as they were related to the vice-president of the society. It was most likely through Tom that the three women learned about the tidal cultivation of rice.

When rice was first grown in South Carolina, planters depended on rainfall to water their crops, but soon discovered that using ponds or reservoirs of fresh water to irrigate the fields yielded larger rice crops. The pond or reservoir system worked well most of the time, except when heavy, sudden rains flooded the irrigation ditches causing great harm to the crop, or when a long drought dried up reservoirs and ponds.

The idea of using the ebb and flow of tidal rivers to flood and drain rice fields was initiated in the Georgetown area around 1758, but because of the labor and expense involved in preparing the fields, its use was not widespread before the revolution. However, the war had caused a disruption to the normal routine of maintaining the ditches and banks on rice plantations, and many planters found their rice fields needed to be completely redone. Since the fields needed to be rebuilt anyway, most planters felt they might as well rebuild them in a way that would improve the yield of their crop. Thus, the tidal cultivation of rice grew in popularity.

There was a considerable amount of work involved in preparing the fields. First, a permanent embankment five feet high and three feet wide at the top, and twelve to fifteen feet wide at the bottom, had to be built. Then a ditch was dug to run along the inner wall of the embankment. At intervals, the outer wall had to be fitted with trunks or gates that let water flow in and out of the ditches, while the inner wall of the embankment had to have drains to keep the water from rising too high in the ditch. The fields had to be divided into squares, each enclosed with banks and watered by a system of internal ditches. In addition, each of the squares had to be subdivided into one hundred or more trenches for sowing.[19] This complicated set of banks and ditches required time and effort, both to build and to maintain, and as such, was available only to those who had an adequate number of enslaved workers.

For tidal cultivation of rice to work, the fields had to be located on a tidal waterway that flowed swiftly, pushing large amounts of fresh water toward the sea — rivers like the Santee and the Waccamaw. Saltwater is heavier than fresh water and, therefore, as the saltwater tide sweeps upriver it travels under an overlying sheet of fresh water, driving the fresh water toward the riverbanks. The trunks or gates in the outer wall of the embankment enabled fresh water to flow into the irrigation ditches when the tide was coming in, and conversely, when the fields needed to be drained, water could flow out at low tide. It was a tricky business, as saltwater could kill or, at the very least, stunt the growth of rice.

Convinced of its efficacy, Rebecca, Harriott, and Fanny adopted the tidal system of rice cultivation on their plantations. While she was seeing to the installation of the new system on her plantation, Rebecca could not have helped to notice her son-in-law was not in the best of health. Tom's leg was still bothering him and he was exhausted, as he had been working long hours to establish his law practice while also trying to manage his rice fields.

As the long, hot summer settled in, the family thought that he should travel to a cooler climate to rest and recover his health. Newport, Rhode Island had long been a favorite retreat for South Carolinians, both as an escape from the heat of summer, and as a place to restore their health. Consequently, at the end of June 1786, in spite of the strain the trip would impose on their finances, Tom, Betsey, and the children, along with Fanny and her son, set sail for Newport, accompanied by a few of their enslaved servants.[20] No doubt while they were gone, Rebecca and Harriott looked after their property.

After spending a little over three months in Newport, the group returned to South Carolina in early November. The long, restful sojourn had done much to restore Tom to good health, and he returned with renewed vigor. It was providential, for on February 20, 1787, the General Assembly of South Carolina elected him governor of the state. As governor, Tom would later preside over the state convention convened to ratify the United States Constitution. On May 23, 1788, South Carolina became the eighth state in the union to do so.

Adoption of the tidal method of cultivating rice created such an abundance of rice in South Carolina that there was a backlog of grain waiting to be milled or "pounded." At this time, the process of removing the outer husk from the grains was done by hand, the rice being pounded in a wooden mortar with a pestle, or by cog mills driven by animals. Planters, of course, could sell their rice unhusked or "rough," but the price was much lower.

Providentially, in 1786 Jonathan Lucas, a skilled millwright from the north of England, immigrated to South Carolina, settled on Shem Creek just north of Charleston, and began to experiment with using wind and water as power sources for mills. Hired by John Bowman in 1787 to improve the output of the rice mill on his Peach Tree Plantation, Lucas devised a mill powered by an undershot waterwheel fed by a millpond. It was hugely successful, allowing Bowman to have his rice cleaned and ready to market in a short amount of time.[21]

Peach Tree Plantation was located on the South Santee River, not far from Washo and Eldorado. It is possible that Rebecca and Fanny visited the plantation and saw the mill in operation.

However, whether they actually saw the mill or just heard about it, they must have been very impressed for, a short time later, Fanny commissioned Jonathan Lucas to build a mill for her on her Washo plantation. It was in operation sometime before August of 1789.[22]

It may have been around this time that Rebecca decided to purchase more land. The timing would have been perfect. The yield of her rice fields had improved as a result of using tidal cultivation, and now, thanks to her daughter's mill, she could have her rice cleaned and shipped off to market in a timely manner. If she could plant more rice, her income would increase substantially. Giving a bond for the land, she purchased a "piece of swamp" from the estate of Sampson Neyle, and a "piece of high land" from Jonah Collins.[23]

The beginning of the year 1789 was a momentous time for the new United States of America, for the country was about to begin the process of choosing the two men who would serve as the first president and vice-president. Under the new constitution, these two men were to be chosen by electors from all thirteen states, and would serve for four years. The electors were chosen in January, and on February 4, 1789, the first electors met and cast their votes. On April 4, Congress officially counted the votes and announced that George Washington had been unanimously elected president and John Adams the vice-president. Their inauguration took place on April 30, 1789.

As the electors were meeting to cast their votes, Thomas Pinckney's two-year term as governor of South Carolina was coming to a close. It was probably with a great sigh of relief that Tom stepped down from office and returned to private life. Now he would have more time to devote to his family, to improving his plantations, and to pursuing his agricultural interests. It is likely that while Tom was serving as governor and spending much of his time in Charleston, Rebecca continued to live at Fairfield, keeping an eye on the rice production there as well as her own at Eldorado. During this time, she may also have been having a house built on her plantation — not the beautiful mansion-house whose crumbling foundations now stand on the property, but a smaller, less grand dwelling place.

Obviously, she was making plans to move to her own plantation, for while in June of 1789 Rebecca was still living at Fairfield,[24] by April of 1790 she was at Eldorado. At the end of a letter dated April 17, 1790 from Charles Cotesworth Pinckney in Charleston to his sister Harriot Charles wrote, "we wish all at Hampton and Eldorado every happiness."[25] In the 1790 census, Rebecca was listed as the head of household and living alone in St. James Santee, with 71 enslaved workers on her property.

Chapter Twelve
The Rice Planter

In addition to settling her husband's estate and establishing a rice plantation, Rebecca had a daughter to raise. When she bought Eldorado in 1784, her daughter Mary was sixteen years old, ready to enter society and begin the process of finding a husband. Rebecca would have wanted to give her daughter every opportunity to mingle in society and would have arranged to spend the "social season" in Charleston, accompanying Mary to the many social events taking place in town, as well as hosting events in her own home.

At some point in 1790, Mary met Colonel William Alston, a wealthy rice planter from the Waccamaw River area near Georgetown. William, thirty-five years old and a widower with five children, was evidently quite taken with 22-year-old Mary, and seeing that his affections were returned, asked her to marry him. Undaunted by the prospect of becoming a stepmother to five children ranging in age from seven to thirteen, Mary accepted his proposal. The two were wed on February 24, 1791.

Although she may have had a few qualms about the number of children Mary was acquiring in the marriage, Rebecca was likely pleased with the match. She may have been even more pleased two months later when her new son-in-law offered to buy the Miles Brewton House from her and her sister. Evidently, William wanted the house as a gift for Mary. Rebecca and Frances accepted the offer, and on April 19, sold the house on King Street to William Alston for £7,000.[1]

As if acquiring five children was not stress enough for Mary, there was more to come. At the beginning of 1791, when George Washington announced his plan to tour the southern cities in the spring, William Alston invited the president to break his journey and dine at Clifton, his plantation on the east bank of the Waccamaw River. Mary had to plan a dinner party grand enough to impress the most important man in the country — a daunting task for a new bride.

However, Mary took it all in stride — she was, after all, Rebecca's daughter. On April 28, 1791, President Washington, his entourage, and selected guests were entertained at Clifton in a style "which the president pronounced to be truly Virginian." This was a high compliment indeed, as Virginians were known for their gracious hospitality. Mary was said to have met the president wearing a "band on her forehead on which was emblazoned, "Hail to the Chief."[2]

A few days later, on May 1, the president, who had accepted an invitation from Harriott Horry to dine at Hampton Plantation, crossed the Santee River with his entourage and was met by Thomas Pinckney, who escorted the party to his sister's house. Washington was acquainted with Tom's brother Charles, whom he had met in the early days of the war, and again at the Constitutional Convention, but this was the first time he had met Tom, though he had heard many good things about him.

When Washington returned to Philadelphia after his southern tour, he learned that the British had decided to exchange diplomatic representatives with the United States. He was pleased, as he believed this was a great step toward gaining the prestige the new nation needed and, moreover, he knew exactly whom he wanted to appoint to fill this important position — a South Carolinian he had met on his tour of the South who was intelligent, had just the right temperament for a diplomat, and who, most importantly, had spent his childhood in England and gone to school there. His name was Thomas Pinckney. In November of 1791, Washington offered Tom the post as the United States' minister to Great Britain.

Tom accepted the nomination, and in mid-January, the Senate confirmed his appointment. While Tom's family and friends were pleased that such an honor had been bestowed on him, his appointment was also viewed with a touch of sadness; Tom and his family would be greatly missed. Eliza, Tom's mother, must have been especially sad to see them leave. She was now sixty-nine years old, and the chances were very good that she would not live to see Tom and his family return. That thought may have even crossed Rebecca's mind as well; though she was only in her mid-fifties, she would have been considered an old woman by the standards of her day.

However, it was Betsey who was the most affected by the appointment. She enjoyed her life in South Carolina. She did not want to leave her home, her family, and her large circle of friends to live in a strange country amid people who had so recently been the "enemy." Betsey, who had managed to keep her spirits up during the difficult years of the war, could not now control her tears.[3] It must have been heartbreaking for Rebecca to see her daughter so distressed.

In February, a welcome distraction occurred, taking everyone's mind off the imminent departure of Betsey and her family. Mary gave birth to her first child, a little girl. She was named Rebecca Brewton Alston after her maternal grandmother but was always called "Brewton." A new grandbaby to fuss over and admire may have been some compensation to Rebecca for temporarily losing four granddaughters and two grandsons when the Pinckney family went to England.[4]

In April, the sad day arrived. Betsey and Tom left for Philadelphia, along with their children and a few enslaved servants, including John Riley, Tom's valet, John's wife, who was Betsey's maid, and a maidservant named Sydney, who was apparently as unhappy to leave South Carolina as her mistress.[5] They were to remain in Philadelphia for several weeks while Tom conferred with government officials and prepared for his new mission. On June 25, they sailed from New Castle, Delaware for England, arriving in London on August 3.

Meanwhile, at the beginning of summer Rebecca, Fanny, and Fanny's son John, now an active eight-year-old, had retreated to Murphy's Island located at the mouth of the South Santee River. Harriott Horry had a rice plantation on the island, but the Motte family and several of their friends and relatives also had summer houses there where they went to enjoy the cool ocean breezes during the long, hot Carolina summers. It had been one of Betsey's favorite places to visit.

It must have seemed very lonely without Betsey and her family on Murphy's Island that summer. Rebecca would surely have missed the sound of her grandchildren's laughter as they ran along the beach, stopping to collect seashells or splashing in the water. While Betsey might not have been there in person, she was there in thought. In August, a few weeks after the Pinckney family arrived in England, Betsey wrote to Mary: "… would you believe it! I have never been in the Park tho I live very near it, or at a play, or any where else & have not the least inclination to go, I have wishd a thousand times to be at Murphy's Island with my dear Mother & Sister."[6]

Although Rebecca and Fanny had their own plantations and were listed in the 1790 census as heads of households on their separate properties, it is possible that Fanny stayed with Rebecca at Eldorado for much of the time, returning to Washo for short periods whenever necessary. It would have been an ideal arrangement. They were kindred spirits — single women with rice plantations to manage and debts to pay — and to have a kindred spirit to discuss problems with and share ideas would have been beneficial to them both.

There was another kindred spirit living close by — Harriott Horry — who was also a single woman with rice plantations to manage. The three women, drawn together by kinship, mutual regard and common interests, formed a very close bond. They also had a close relationship with Charles Cotesworth Pinckney, Harriott's brother, who handled their legal affairs. Just as they had confidence in Charles's ability to manage their legal and financial affairs, Charles had confidence in their management skills, and often entrusted them to carry out special commissions for him.

While Tom was in England, it was the four of them — Charles, Rebecca, Harriott, and Fanny — who looked after his interests in South Carolina. Charles had Tom's power of attorney, and it was he who took care of Tom's finances, legal matters, and directed affairs at Fairfield. However, Charles had a busy law practice and properties of his own to manage, and he was quite happy to leave some of the details at Fairfield to Rebecca, Harriott, and Fanny.

For example, in February of 1794, Charles wrote to his brother: I "planted you out last Christmas a Vineyard of about a quarter of an Acre between your first and second gate, on the declivity with a southern aspect — My Sister, Mrs. Motte and Mrs. Middleton promise to attend to filling the ground with trees and trimming up the young oaks."[7]

In September of 1794, the weather dealt rice planters along the Santee River a severe blow. Heavy rains caused flooding on the river that ruined the entire rice crop on Harriott's plantations, as well as the crop at Fairfield. At Eldorado, Rebecca was dismayed to learn that instead of the 450 barrels of rice she was expecting, she would make less than 100. Only Fanny at Washo escaped ruin, as she was able to make 800 barrels of rice out of the 1,000 barrels she expected. That was not the end of it. After the floods in September, two or three unusually cold evenings in October seriously threatened the rice meant for seed.[8]

Rebecca, who was depending on her rice crop to pay her debts, must have been very disappointed that fall. However,

Rebecca Brewton Motte

her spirits were uplifted in late October when she and Fanny received a visit at Eldorado from Charles Cotesworth who brought good news with him: Rebecca's largest bond for the land she had purchased from Sampson Neyle's estate had been cancelled, and the executors had told Charles they did not require any payment on the second, smaller bond until January 1796.[9] What a relief it must have been to Rebecca to have her largest bond paid off, and, considering the paucity of this year's rice crop, to know that payment on the second bond was deferred until the sale of next year's crop.

A few hours later, as Rebecca, Fanny, and Charles were still celebrating, a communication from England reached them with news so shocking it destroyed their pleasure — Betsey was dead. She had been "seized with a painful disorder" during the summer, and the family, instead of taking their usual summer trip, had stayed in town waiting for her to regain her strength.[10] Sadly, Betsey had grown weaker instead of stronger, and on the 24th of August, she had passed away at the age of thirty-two. Regrettably, it had taken a little over two months for the news to reach her family and friends in South Carolina.

Such unexpected news would have stunned the three of them. Rebecca and Fanny knew how Betsey had dreaded going to England, and the fact that she had died so far from home and the rest of her family added to their grief. However, in spite of their obvious distress over Betsey's death, both Rebecca and Fanny would have known from personal experience that life does not stop because of the loss of a loved one. They had responsibilities and obligations to fulfill, and they needed to keep moving forward. By the time Charles Cotesworth returned to Charleston and wrote to his brother on November 4, he reported: "Mrs. Motte and Mrs. Middleton have in some measure recovered their tranquility."[11]

A few weeks later, Alice Izard, the wife of Ralph Izard, was returning to South Carolina from Philadelphia, and was forced by impassable roads to seek shelter at Charleywood Plantation located at the head of the Wando River. The plantation was owned by Charles Cotesworth Pinckney and his law-partner Ned Rutledge, who had bought it after the war as an investment. In a letter to her husband, Mrs. Izard wrote, "At Charleywood I unexpectedly met Mrs. Motte, & Mrs. J. Middleton who were in better spirits than I could have expected. They were most friendly to me & I dined, slept & breakfasted there with them. The next morning they went to Santee, & I came to Town..."[12] Rebecca and Fanny had most likely gone to Charleywood at Charles's request to undertake some business for him.

Meanwhile, Tom, in addition to losing his beloved wife, was having financial troubles. His salary as minister to Great Britain was, unfortunately, not large enough to cover all his expenses. As Charles pointed out to him in a letter, "...from all your Letters it appears that with the utmost Economy you spend five hundred pounds Sterling annually above your Salary."[13] Normally this difference would have been made up by the sale of the rice crop at Fairfield, but because the year's crop was ruined, that was not possible.

Fortunately, Tom's female relatives were prepared to come to his rescue. Rebecca was not in a position to help Tom, but her sister and Fanny were. Charles, who was the attorney for both Fanny and Frances, put the following propositions to his brother in a letter written in October, before the news of Betsey's death had reached South Carolina:

> Mrs. Pinckney [Frances] with great kindness & altogether of her own Motion offered to lend you five hundred pounds of the Money she has in Mr. Manning's hands [probably her agent in London]; If out of too great delicacy you wish not to accept this, what think you of the following plan. One of the Bonds of John Middleton's Estate to Mr. Lowndes for twelve hundred pounds is now the property of Mrs. Pinckney; If Mrs. Middleton [Fanny] is not called upon this Year for the payment of any part of the principal, as she will make Eight hundred Barrels of Rice, she proposes to lend you two hundred, & Mrs. Pinckney very

chearfully agrees to call for no part of the principal this Year, nor indeed for the interest without it is convenient for Mrs. Middleton to pay it.[14]

Charles had then asked his brother to let him know which proposal he wished to accept. However, now that they had learned of Betsey's death, Charles, Rebecca, and Fanny decided they should not wait for Tom's reply, but should, instead, send the two hundred barrels of rice to him as soon as the rice could be milled.[15]

The year 1794 had not been a particularly good one for Rebecca, and she must have hoped that 1795 would prove more promising. Regrettably, as the new year began, some distressing news reached her: Frances was ill and in a great deal of pain. Rebecca would have gone immediately to her sister's side, remembering that once before Frances had been taken ill, causing concern in the family, but she had recovered. However, the illness did not go away, it lingered and Frances did not get better. She died on April 4, 1795, at the age of 61.[16] Frances was Rebecca's last link to her childhood, the one person left who had shared the happiness and sorrows of youth with her. Her passing would have filled Rebecca with the deepest sorrow and created a void that would be difficult to fill.

Meanwhile, as Rebecca was dealing with the loss of her sister in South Carolina, in London, Tom, coping as best as he could with Betsey's death, had been given a special assignment. The president had asked him to go to Spain to negotiate a treaty establishing the border between the United States and the Spanish territory of West Florida which, at that time, encompassed most of the Florida panhandle along with the gulf coasts of the present-day states of Alabama, Mississippi, and Louisiana.

Leaving his oldest son at school in London and depositing the rest of his children in school in Paris under the watchful eye of the new minister to France, James Monroe and his wife, Tom journeyed to the Spanish capital, reaching Madrid on June 28. The negotiations dragged on through the summer, however, and it was not until October 27 that the Treaty of San Lorenzo, or the Pinckney Treaty as it was sometimes called, was signed. The treaty defined the border between the United States and Spanish West Florida, gave the United States the right of navigation on the Mississippi River, and access to the port of New Orleans. The treaty was immensely popular in America, and, most unusual for the time, was hailed with joy by both political parties — the Federalists and the Republicans.

While he was in Spain negotiating the treaty, Tom had come to a decision. He wanted to go home, look after his property, pursue his agricultural interests, and reunite his children with their family in South Carolina. As a result, in October, as the negotiations were coming to a close, Tom wrote the president asking to be recalled from his post by mid-June of 1796. Washington reluctantly agreed, but it was not until July of 1796 that his replacement, Rufus King, reached London. Wanting to wait until the sickly season had passed in South Carolina, Tom and his family did not sail for home until the 17th of October.

Tom anticipated a bittersweet homecoming, as he explained in a letter to Fanny in August:

> Mr. King my successor is arrived & has been presented at Court; I am therefore once more my own Master & only waiting for the autumnal equinox to pass in order to set out to restore to you & our dear Mother [Rebecca] our little flock. I sincerely hope they will prove a consolation to her & that her mind will be so occupied by them that it will dwell less forcibly on the scenes of our irreparable loss — I anxiously desire & yet I dread the approach of the hour which will restore to us what remains of our Families; for what object will present itself to me which will not remind me of the happiness I once enjoyed in the society of one who doubled all my pleasures and alleviated all my sorrows? And when I reflect on the happiness she would have enjoyed in such a meeting, the misery attending her absence is not to be described.[17]

It is not clear when Tom first informed his family in South Carolina that he planned to return home, but whenever he did so, the news would have made them all very happy — especially

Rebecca, longing to see her grandchildren and to determine for herself how they were coping with the loss of their mother.

In the meantime, Rebecca had had some good luck. She found a buyer for her Mount Joseph Plantation and on September 2, 1795, she sold it to Elnathan Haskell, the son-in-law of Colonel William Thomson of nearby Belleville Plantation.[18] Mount Joseph was possibly the last piece of Rebecca's inherited property to be sold, meaning that the remainder of her husband's debts would have to be satisfied by the rice crop at Eldorado.[19]

On September 17, 1796, as Tom and his family were preparing to return home, George Washington announced that he was retiring from public life — he would not run for a third term as president. The Federalists and the Democratic-Republicans, suspecting that the president might not seek re-election, had already decided who would be their presidential and vice-presidential candidates. Rebecca must have been greatly surprised when she learned that Tom had been chosen by the Federalist party as their candidate for vice-president. He would run with John Adams, the Federalist nominee for president, against Thomas Jefferson and Aaron Burr, the Democratic-Republican nominees. Since Tom left England on October 17, it is quite likely that he had not heard that Washington was retiring, and that he and Adams were running for the two highest offices in the country.

The electoral procedure at this time was ripe for manipulation. Each elector cast two votes and the candidate with the most votes became president, and the one with the second highest number became vice-president. Federalists unfriendly to Adams would have preferred the ticket to be reversed, with Pinckney as president and Adams as vice-president, and to bring this plan to fruition, they decided to withhold some votes from Adams to make Pinckney president instead. However, when Adams's friends discovered the plot, they decided to withhold votes from Pinckney to ensure that Adams became president.

By the time Tom and his family arrived in Charleston on December 17, the electors had been chosen, and voting had started. When the votes were officially counted on February 9, 1797, it appeared that the Federalists had outmaneuvered themselves. They had managed to elect John Adams president but had withheld too many votes from Tom Pinckney and, consequently, had elected their strongest political opponent, Thomas Jefferson, as vice-president.

Tom was most likely not greatly upset by the results of the election, although he may have thought that having a president from one party and a vice-president from the opposing party was not particularly good for the country. However, he was back in South Carolina where he wanted to be, and could now settle down to the life of a gentleman planter and pursue his agricultural interests.

It must have been a joyous occasion for Rebecca when she was re-united with her grandchildren. She had not seen them for over four years. The two older ones, Tom Jr., and Elizabeth, were now sixteen and fifteen years of age respectively, and little Cotesworth, (Charles Cotesworth Pinckney, II) who had been only three when the family left for England, was now a sturdy lad of seven. They would have so much to tell about their lives in England. Those who had gone to Paris while their father was in Spain would also regale Rebecca with stories of the French capital. No doubt, just as Tom had hoped, their presence helped console her for the loss of her daughter.

When Tom returned to Fairfield, his top priority would have been to see his children settled. His sons needed to be in school — the oldest to prepare for entrance into Princeton, and the younger to continue his education. Tom may have conferred with Fanny, who had a school-aged son, on a possible

Rebecca Brewton Motte

school or tutors for both of them. His daughters also needed to continue their education, but he was quite willing to leave their upbringing in the capable hands of his mother-in-law, who had successfully raised three very accomplished daughters.

As soon as Tom had his children settled, he began to implement some of the changes he wanted to make on his plantation. It must have been an exciting time for Rebecca. She liked to be busy and involved in whatever was happening around her and, now, in addition to her usual activities, she had her granddaughters to raise, and since Tom probably shared his plans and ideas with her, she would have been a party to the changes he wanted to make at Fairfield.

As the days and weeks passed, Tom and Fanny, who had known one another for years and were good friends, evidently discovered that the fondness they had for each other as sister-in-law and brother-in-law was developing into something deeper. As a result, Tom asked Fanny to marry him, and Fanny, who had once refused an offer of marriage from Pierce Butler, accepted. Rebecca must have been delighted — it was, in many ways, a perfect match.

When Tom and Fanny decided to marry, they agreed on the distribution of their property among their three sons: John Middleton Jr., Thomas Pinckney Jr., and Charles Cotesworth Pinckney, II. Washo Plantation and Fairfield Plantation would go to John, junior and Tom, junior respectively — the oldest Middleton and Pinckney sons. The couple decided to give Aukland, Tom's plantation on the Ashpoo River, to Cotesworth.[20] They also concluded they wanted their sons to take possession of their plantations as soon as they were married. Therefore, when Tom Jr. married, Fanny and Tom would leave Fairfield Plantation and take up residence at Eldorado with Rebecca — a plan that would have certainly met with her approval.

American Patriot and Successful Rice Planter

It is not known what size house Rebecca was living in at Eldorado, but it was probably not very large or grand, and she may have decided that, since Tom and Fanny would eventually be living there, it was time to build a proper owner's mansion on the property. Many believe that Rebecca and Tom designed the house at Eldorado together. Hannibal, Joe, Daniel, and Chance, the skilled enslaved carpenters at Eldorado, along with the enslaved carpenters from Fairfield, completed most of the house's construction.[21]

The new house stood on a sandy mound that jutted out into the rice fields and was surrounded by live oaks and magnolia trees. On the side of the house that faced the river, there was a portico similar to the one at Fairfield. It was a spacious and airy house with lofty ceilings and expanded wings that allowed for the strategic placement of windows to take advantage of the breeze from the river. Construction on the house most likely began sometime during the summer of 1797, but it is not clear exactly when it was completed and when Rebecca was able to move into it.[22]

Since Fanny and Tom were planning to get married in October, Rebecca and the rest of the family would have come to Charleston at some point in September to begin preparations for the wedding and social events being held to celebrate it. At the same time that Rebecca was planning Fanny's wedding, Harriott Horry was arranging for the wedding of her daughter Harriott to Frederick Rutledge, the son of John and Elizabeth Rutledge.

The Horry-Rutledge wedding was held on October 11, no doubt with Rebecca and the rest of the family in attendance. Then, just a little over a week later, on the evening of October 19, 1797, Frances Motte Middleton and Thomas Pinckney were married. Leaving their children and plantations in Rebecca's capable hands, the couple set off a week later for Philadelphia. Tom had been elected to represent South Carolina in the United

States House of Representatives and Congress was scheduled to meet there toward the end of the month.

November found Rebecca and her four Pinckney granddaughters still in Charleston. Maria Alston, Mary's stepdaughter, was to marry Sir John Nesbitt, the son of a Scottish nobleman, in mid-November, and Maria had asked the four Pinckney sisters to be her bridesmaids. Mary was also expecting a baby in November, and Rebecca was planning to remain in town until after the birth.

By the time Rebecca and her granddaughters were able to leave town and return to Eldorado, the Christmas season was approaching, and it was time to begin preparing for the holidays. Sadly, in the midst of all the excitement and preparations for Christmas, nine-year-old Becky, Tom's youngest daughter, fell seriously ill. In spite of all they could do Becky died on Christmas Eve, casting the family into deep mourning. The fact that he was away in Philadelphia when his daughter died must have made the blow even harder for Tom to bear.

While Tom and Fanny were in Philadelphia, Rebecca looked after the four plantations the couple owned in the Santee area. She sent Tom an account every week of the state of each of the plantations: how many barrels of rice had been produced, the number of acres under cultivation, the work that needed to be done, and so forth — information she received from the reports sent to her by the overseers. The one exception was Fairfield — Mr. Talbot, the overseer there, had such illegible handwriting that Rebecca thought it best to travel to Fairfield each week to get his report in person. Keeping in mind that she was charged with the education of her granddaughters, Rebecca set sixteen-year-old Elizabeth to work writing most of the letters to Tom — excellent training for a young lady destined to be a plantation mistress.[23]

April arrived, and Fanny and Tom were still in Philadelphia. It was planting season and, there was a new method of planting corn that Tom wanted to try. He sent the instructions to Rebecca, who saw that the planting was done as he wished. Rebecca also sent Hannibal, her best carpenter, to inspect a new kind of water mill being built on one of the nearby plantations, so he would know how to frame the one Tom wanted built at Fairfield. When she discovered that the wheel on the rice mill at Fairfield was too warped to function properly, Rebecca contacted Johnathan Lucas, the millwright, to make arrangements for him to replace it.[24]

There was always something on one or the other of the plantations that needed her attention, it seemed, but it does not appear that Rebecca ever felt overwhelmed by any of it. That was fortunate, for Tom would continue to represent the state of South Carolina in the House of Representatives for four more years and would continue to rely on Rebecca to look after the family plantations while he and Fanny were absent.

In 1803, Thomas Pinckney Jr. married Eliza Izard, and took possession of Fairfield, at which time Tom and Fanny came to live at Eldorado. However, there had been an addition to their family. In 1800, Fanny had given birth to a baby boy — Edward Rutledge Pinckney — and the house would now be filled with the sound of running feet and childish laughter. The following year, Fanny, at the age of 41, found that she was pregnant again, and although the pregnancy came with great risks, the baby — a little girl named Mary — was born without complications.

The family at Eldorado soon settled into a comfortable pattern. They spent the summers on Murphy's Island or Sullivan's Island and divided the rest of the year between Eldorado and the house that Tom and Fanny had built on George Street in Ansonborough — at that time a suburb of Charleston. Rebecca did not always accompany them to town, choosing instead to remain at Eldorado with one or two of her Alston granddaughters as company. She continued to see Harriott Horry, now a grandmother herself, and the two families remained close, frequently exchanging visits and celebrating holidays together.

Tom and Fanny may have resided at Eldorado, but Eldorado was Rebecca's plantation, and she continued to manage it on her own. She was still paying off her debts, and in spite of fluctuations in the price of rice, the quirks of the weather, and the disruptions to commerce caused by the Napoleonic Wars, she was making progress. In 1806 she wrote to Mary, "Now I have told you all the news I know of. I will inform you about my crop. I have a better prospect of a good crop than I ever had; there was more pains taken in planting; all my seed rice was hand picked and if rice is but a good price next year I shall pay off all my debts — I hope."[25] Unfortunately, that hope was not realized. Rebecca may have been able to pay the debts she had incurred in establishing Eldorado, but claims against her husband's estate would continue to plague her for the rest of her life.

In 1807, Rebecca celebrated her seventieth birthday. At a time when the life expectancy of a person who survived childhood was only fifty-five, she would have been considered very old, indeed. Her health was beginning to decline, however, and she was not as agile as she had once been — perhaps a touch of arthritis or rheumatism. She declined making a trip to visit one of her married granddaughters in February of 1807 because, as she explained to Mary, "I am so lame it would be a great undertaking for me."[26]

At the beginning of 1809, Rebecca was taken ill and confined to her bed. Harriott, who was in Charleston at the time, pressed her brother continually for information about Rebecca's condition. By the end of February, he was able to assure her that "Mrs. Motte continues to mend slowly." Two days he later wrote again: "Mrs. Motte sets up the greatest part of the day but has not yet left her chamber."[27]

American Patriot and Successful Rice Planter

While Rebecca was slowly recovering from her illness, tensions between the United States and Great Britain over trade issues and the harassment of American shipping by the Royal Navy were increasing. The situation grew steadily worse, and on June 18, 1812, President Madison asked Congress for a declaration of war against Great Britain. The president then reached out to Thomas Pinckney, offering him command of the Southern Division of the United States Army with the rank of major general. Tom was now sixty-one years old and would probably have preferred to remain at home, but the call to duty was strong, and he accepted the post.

His military duties took him away from home for much time during the war, leaving others, once again, to manage his property for him. This time it would be his sons, for Rebecca had reached the stage in life when, instead of reaching out to help others, she needed help herself. Mentally she was probably as sharp as ever, but she was slowing down and was not physically able to oversee her plantation as she would have liked. It was Cotesworth, now twenty-three years old and looking after his father's plantation on nearby Cedar Island, who came to her assistance.[28]

Rebecca spent her last years at Eldorado, in the lovely, spacious house she had helped design and build, with Cotesworth in close attendance. He helped her manage the plantation and also deal with claims still being brought against Jacob's estate. Rebecca was determined that her children receive their full inheritance from their father, unencumbered by any obligations to his estate. To ensure the matter, she stipulated in her will that all her field hands be kept together "and employed upon my Plantation ... until the Crop produced thereon shall yield a sum adequate to the satisfaction of all my debts ... among which debts I reckon as the principal one what is due to my children" for their interest in the wharf in Charleston. This was the wharf which she had sold, with their permission, to help pay Jacob's creditors. It was the only part of their father's estate they had not yet received. Tom, Fanny, and Mary would eventually be paid £1,666, 14 shillings each, in compensation.[29]

Rebecca Motte was a calm, caring, and courteous person by nature who met life's challenges with courage and determination. She died on January 10, 1815, at the age of 77, and lies buried in the graveyard at St. Philip's Episcopal Church in Charleston. There in 1903, a monument was erected in her honor by the Rebecca Motte Chapter of The Daughters of the American Revolution.

Epilogue

After her inspiring visit to the site of Fort Motte, Elizabeth Ellet began her quest for more information about Rebecca Motte by interviewing her grandchildren, great-grandchildren, and people with whom she had been connected. Mrs. Ellet was pleasantly surprised to discover that Rebecca's role in the Siege of Fort Motte was generally well-known in her home state of South Carolina — which had not been the case with the other women she had studied.[1] That was not too surprising, Mrs. Ellet would have realized. The capture of Fort Motte had been an important victory for the Americans, and the siege and the pivotal role that Rebecca played in the fort's capture had been well documented in contemporary histories, biographies, and memoirs.

Rebecca, Mrs. Ellet was told, was fond of entertaining those around her with stories about the interesting people she had met and the exciting events she had witnessed during the Revolutionary War. Her grandchildren and great-grandchildren said that, while they had enjoyed listening to all her stories, they had, most of all, loved to hear her talk of the exciting scene of setting fire to her own house. Her descendants, Mrs. Ellet found, were proud of the graciousness and generosity she had shown to British soldiers during the war, and the dignity which she displayed in the face of taunts by the enemy. By their manner of speaking, Mrs. Ellet concluded that, besides being proud of their grandmother or great-grandmother, they also held her in a great deal of affection.[2]

After giving Mrs. Ellet information about Rebecca's background — who her parents were, her husband's family, number of children, etc. — her descendants passed on another very interesting piece of information. Although they were a little vague on details, the gist of what they remembered was this:

Rebecca had borrowed money to buy a rice plantation and the necessary enslaved labor to work it; built a small house on the property for herself and became an independent rice planter not only paying off her debts, but the debts left by her husband, ensuring that her children were left with an unencumbered inheritance. She accomplished all this in spite of the fact that many people had told her it could not be done.[3] Mrs. Ellet was astonished.

But why were Rebecca's achievements considered so noteworthy by her descendants and Mrs. Ellet? Rebecca never amassed a huge fortune from her rice plantation. Eldorado was not large — only 400 or so acres. Moreover, she was not the only successful female rice planter in South Carolina. Harriott and Fanny were also successful rice planters with multiple plantations to manage, any one of which was probably larger than Eldorado.

Harriott and Fanny, however, had not chosen to be plantation managers, it was a role that had been thrust upon them by the deaths of their husbands. Besides, the plantations they were managing, for the most part, did not belong to them, but were part of their children's inheritance. They were simply acting as caretakers of the properties until their children came of age.

Rebecca was unique in that she *chose* to become a plantation owner — did not assume the role because circumstances prescribed it. She sold everything that she had been given — all the property she had inherited from her husband and her brother — to pay her husband's debts and established a successful rice plantation entirely on her own — and that was truly noteworthy. Few women of her time would have had the courage to do it.

Mrs. Ellet was so impressed with what Rebecca had accomplished, that even though these accomplishments had nothing to do with the American Revolution, she decided to include them in her book in the chapter about Rebecca Motte. It illustrated, she wrote, "her singular energy, resolution, and strength of principle.[4] Rebecca Motte, Mrs. Ellet concluded, was a remarkable woman. "Her fame is, indeed, a rich inheritance," she wrote, "for of one like her the land of her birth may well be proud!"[5]

Addendum
Fort Motte — Then and Now

By the time Elizabeth Ellet visited the site of Fort Motte in the late 1840s, sixty-five years had passed since the siege, and the countryside had changed. Cotton had become the all-important cash crop in the area, and the railroad now connected the midlands and the backcountry with the city of Charleston. The main rail line stretching 136 miles from Charleston to Hamburg had been completed in 1833, and by 1842 a branch line to Columbia had been added. Departing from the mainline at Branchville, the new rail line veered northward, making its way to Columbia by way of Orangeburg, St. Matthews, and a little town that developed along the tracks not far from the former Mount Joseph Plantation. The local residents, who had not forgotten the exciting events that had taken place on Rebecca's plantation in May of 1781, called the aspiring town Fort Motte.

Changes had also come to the former Mount Joseph Plantation by the 1840s. Over the years Rebecca's house had either been destroyed and another built in its place, or her house had been renovated and enlarged, forming the core of the house now standing on the property. In 1849 the historian and artist Benson Lossing came to the plantation to gather material for his book *Pictorial Field-Book of the American Revolution*. According to Lossing, the plantation was then owned by William H. Love, and his house was "built nearly upon the site of Mrs. Motte's mansion." Lossing then added, "The well used by that patriotic lady is still there ... and from it to the house there is a slight hollow, which indicates the place of a covered way, dug for the protection of the soldiers when procuring water."[1]

Time and the Civil War brought more changes to the former Mount Joseph Plantation. After the war, the eastern part of the old plantation, which included the site of Fort Motte, was owned by the Moye family.² In 1868 James Jamieson rented a room "from the men on the fort Motte plantation of Mrs. Moyes which they have rented for this year" and opened a school for African Americans. In a letter to the Freedmen's Bureau in Columbia, Jamieson described the location of his school as being two miles from the railroad depot at Fort Motte and about 200 yards from the old fort.³

An 1870 plat shows the land to the west of the site of Fort Motte as being part of a large tract of land owned by Dr. Thomas J. Goodwyn. To the east and adjacent to Dr. Goodwyn's land, the plat shows an "Old House" on Mrs. Moye's land — presumably, the house that had belonged to William Love and the site of the old fort mentioned by James Jamieson.⁴

At this time, the little town of Fort Motte was growing. In 1875 it was incorporated, and in 1907 it boasted a post office, several stores and two banks. As the town flourished, the house on the "Old Fort Motte" tract, or, as it was sometimes called, the "Moye Place," had been abandoned and left to ruin. By 1909 there was little to nothing left of the house. The Moultrie Chapter of The Daughters of the American Revolution, fearing that the site of Fort Motte was in danger of being lost to posterity, placed a stone monument on the property to mark the location of Rebecca's house. The ceremony took place on May 12, 1909 — 128 years to the day after the Americans had captured the fort.

In 1918 the acreage containing the site of Rebecca's house came into the possession of the Wannamaker family. It is now owned by Luther Wannamaker who found the stone monument erected by the DAR tipped on its side, having been disturbed by the roots of a large tree growing nearby. He had the tree removed and the monument repositioned on a concrete slab to ensure its stability and has meticulously maintained and preserved the acreage ever since.

The town of Fort Motte has ceased to exist — the construction of Interstate 26 having sounded its death knell. Driving through the rolling countryside today, travelers will see a sign at a crossroad saying Fort Motte, but there will be nothing there but woods, fields, and the ruins of a few vacant buildings. Now only freight trains roll along the tracks, passing by the site of the old depot and the vanished town which in bygone days had been a shipping point for cotton and timber.

The view from the site of the fort, while not the same as the one Ellet viewed in the late 1840s, is still magnificent. To the north is Congaree National Park, occupying the forested floodplain of the Congaree River, a thick growth of trees replacing the fields of broom grass, corn, or cotton seen in Ellet's day. It is a peaceful setting. Bees buzz in the wildflowers that fill the meadow, and the surrounding woods are home to a variety of birds. The monument stands on the crest of the hill surrounded by a rail fence marking the site of Fort Motte — a silent memorial to the exciting events that took place there 240 years ago.

In 2003 Steven D. Smith, Research Professor at the University of South Carolina and former Director of the South Carolina Institute of Archaeology and Anthropology, received permission from Luther Wannamaker to conduct archaeological excavations at the site. During the past eighteen years, he and his team have located the fort and the footprint of Rebecca's house. The people responsible for the placement of the DAR monument, apparently, knew exactly where to place it because the monument sits squarely on the site of the plantation house — near the base of one of its chimneys. The archaeologists have also located the mound where the Americans placed their cannon, the various campsites used by both sides, the farmhouse where Rebecca and her female relations took refuge, and the approach trench dug by the Patriots during the siege.

Today Fort Motte is listed as an archaeological site on the Register of Historic Places. It first appeared on the register in

American Patriot and Successful Rice Planter

1972, but the site only included the five acres surrounding the DAR monument. In 2006, as a result of the work done by Steve Smith and his team, the 1972 nomination was revised to include the entire Fort Motte battlefield, and on November 17, 2006, the revised nomination was approved. The Fort Motte battlefield is now recognized as a site of national importance.

The capture of Fort Motte by the Americans was an important event in May of 1781 as it was instrumental in forcing the British to abandon their outposts in the backcountry and eventually led to the end of the British occupation of the South. However, the Siege of Fort Motte is also significant today because it is, as Steve Smith has called it, "an archetypal battle of the Revolution in South Carolina."[5]

The Siege of Fort Motte truly encapsulates the Revolution as it occured in the South. Most of the groups involved in the war are represented: the Continental Army, British, and Hessian soldiers, Patriot and Loyalist militia, women and children, and enslaved workers. Although it is not known whether they were present at the Siege of Fort Motte, there were Catawba Indians and free Blacks in Marion's brigade, and therefore, these two groups may have also taken part. In addition, two legendary figures were present: Francis Marion, the "Swamp Fox," and Henry "Light-Horse Harry" Lee.

War brings out the best and the worst in human behavior, and this duality is also apparent at the Siege of Fort Motte. According to 18th-century rules of engagement, by refusing to surrender when asked a second time, Lieutenant McPherson stood in great danger of losing his life and was completely at the mercy of the Americans. He was fortunate, for as Lee wrote in his memoirs, "Mercy was extended, although policy commanded death, and the obstinacy of McPherson warranted it. Powerfully as the present occasion called for punishment, and rightfully as it might have been inflicted, not a drop of blood was shed, nor any part of the enemy's baggage taken."[6]

After the surrender, the British officers followed their captors back to the farmhouse where they all enjoyed a "sumptuous dinner" provided by Rebecca. This gallant treatment of the enemy stands in sharp contrast to the treatment meted out to some of the Loyalist prisoners. For many Americans, the war was personal, bitter, and vengeful, and at the Siege of Fort Motte, several members of the militia and the Continental Army allowed their desire for revenge to cloud their judgment, resulting in the summary execution of three men.

As Steve Smith has said: "Fort Motte history has everything a student of the war in South Carolina could want — legends, heroes and heroines, eighteenth-century honor and gallantry, contradictory eyewitness accounts, and despicable injustice."[7] We could even add romance to the list, for it is highly likely that Fanny Motte and John Middleton fell in love during the siege.

It was great drama and Rebecca Motte had played a principal role in this great drama for it had been "her own happy thought of the East Indian arrows hidden away on the top shelf of her wardrobe"[8] that had facilitated the capture of the fort. It is no wonder that she loved telling the story over and over again, and it is no wonder that the story has survived over the centuries.

Steve Smith has summed it up very well: "There were many other battles more costly and bloody, but few combine the common elements of American Revolutionary War history and myth like Fort Motte. In that sense, and from the perspective of historic preservation, Fort Motte is not only a Revolutionary War battlefield, it represents a traditional place in the American experience."[9]

Chapter Notes

Prologue

1. Ellet, *The Women of the American Revolution, Vol. II*, 68.

2. Ibid., 72.

Chapter One

1. *South Carolina Gazette*: July 22, 1745, Miles Brewton Obituary.

2. Hotten, *List of People Who Went From Great Britain to the American Plantations 1600-1700*, 297. There was no standardized spelling at this time and people often spelled their own names differently at different times. Bruton was just another way of spelling Brewton.

3. Salley, "Col. Miles Brewton and Some of his Descendants," South Carolina History and Genealogy Magazine (SCHGM), 128. Goldsmiths were also referred to as "goldsmith-bankers."

4. Ibid., 128-130.

5. Ibid., 128.

6. The ages of Mary Loughton's daughters are based on Anne's tombstone in St. Philip's Graveyard which states that she died February 29, 1760 in the 38th year of her life and the marriage of Mary to William Matthews in November 1736. Since the average age for a girl to marry was between eighteen and twenty-four, Mary was most likely born around 1716.

7. Smith and Smith. *The Dwelling Houses of Charleston, South Carolina*, 26. Miles Brewton owned at least two house lots on Church Street, near his own house on the southwest corner of Tradd and Church Streets. In 1730 he had a house built for his son Robert at 71 Church Street and on the lot next door he had a house built for his daughter Mary. In the deed of gift to his daughter dated 1733, Miles wrote that his son Robert was then living in the house next door.

8. Edgar and Bailey, *Biographical Directory of the South Carolina House of Representatives, Volume II, The Commons House of Assembly*, 98. We know that Robert Brewton served as a vestryman for St. Philip's Parish from 1733-1734 and that he was elected to represent St. Philip's Parish, Charleston, and served

from 1733-1736 and again from 1736-1739. In those days residence in the parish that you represented was not a requirement. Robert could have been elected to represent St. Philip's and then moved to Christ Church and still been able to hold his seat in the legislature. However, vestrymen needed to live in the parish. Robert was a vestryman at Christ Church from 1739-1742 and again from 1744-1745. He also represented Christ Church in the legislature from 1739-1742.

9. Salley, "Col. Miles Brewton," 131-132. The dates for the births of Anne and Susannah are unknown so the dates given are approximate. The *South Carolina Gazette* of Thursday, September 11, 1755, announced the death of Miss Susannah Brewton and described her as being a young lady who possessed "all those qualifications that could render her respectable" which suggests that she had made her appearance in society and was at least fifteen or sixteen years of age.

10. Edgar and Bailey, *Biographical Directory*, 98.

11. Salley, "Col. Miles Brewton," 140-141

12. Wills and Miscellaneous Probate Records for William Loughton, 1671-1868. Wills, Vol 1-2, 1671-1731.

13. Salley, "Col. Miles Brewton," 131.

14. Ibid., 131. The obituary is from the *South Carolina Gazette* dated September 11, 1755.

15. Description of Rebecca Motte by one of her great-grandchildren from a manuscript written in 1876 as quoted in the History of American Women Blog. www.womenhistoryblog.com/2009/01/rebecca-brewton-motte.html.

16. Rebecca Brewton Motte (RBM) to Mary Motte Alston, September 10, 1806 in *Alston, Pringle, Frost Papers (28/630/2)* South Carolina Historical Society (SCHS). "B" is Rebecca Brewton Alston, the oldest child of Mary Motte Alston and William Alston. In her letters to Mary Rebecca often refers to her granddaughter as Brewton.

17. Manuscript in *Motte Collection (30-40)* SCHS

18. Eliza Lucas Pinckney (ELP) to Thomas Pinckney (TP), 4 October 1780 in *The Papers of Eliza Lucas Pinckney and Harriott Pinckney Horry Digital Edition.*

19. DAR Program from the Unveiling of a Tablet to Rebecca Brewton Motte at St. Philip's Church, May 9, 1903.

20. Lee, *The Revolutionary War Memoirs of General Henry Lee*, 349.

American Patriot and Successful Rice Planter

Chapter Two

1. Edgar and Bailey, *Biographical Directory*, 481.

2. Ibid., 481.

3. Webber, "The Register of Christ Church Parish," SCHGM, XXI, Vol 21, No. 3, 105.

4. Edgar and Bailey, *Biographical Directory*, 481.

5. Ibid., 326.

6. Ibid., 482.

7. Ibid., 478.

8. Ibid., 479.

9. Ibid., 479.

10. Smith and Smith, *Dwelling Houses of Charleston, South Carolina*, 30.

11. Ibid., 26 -29.

12. South Carolina. General Assembly. Commons House et al, *The Journal of the Commons House of Assembly 1752-1754*, xi.

13. Ibid., xii. While the amount Motte owed the Treasury was £90,000 in South Carolina money it was only approximately £12,850 in British pounds sterling — the exchange rate being around 7 to 1.

14. South Carolina. General Assembly. Commons House et al, *The Journal of the Commons House*, xii.

Chapter Three

1. National Register of Historic Places Inventory and Nomination Form for Fairfield Plantation. http://www.nationalregister.sc.gov.

2. Russell, "Life in the Southern Colonies" part 1 of 3 in *Journal of the American Revolution* (website: allthingsliberty.com/2013/01/life-in-the-Southern-Colonies-part-1-of-3/.

3. Salley, *Col. Miles Brewton.*" 151.

4. Hopkins, *The Greatest Killer: Smallpox in History*, 244.

5. Krawczynski, "Smith, Benjamin" *South Carolina Encyclopedia*, www.scencyclopedia.org/sce/entries/smith-benjamin/

6. Ibid.

7. South Carolina. General Assembly. Commons House et al., *Journal of the Commons House, 1759-1760 Part I*, 184.

8. Sellers, *Charleston Business on the Eve of the American Revolution*, 178.

9. Ibid., 188.

10. Williams, Frances Leigh, *A Founding Family, the Pinckneys of South Carolina*, 29.

11. Salley, in "Col. Miles Brewton and Some of His Descendants" lists 7 children for Rebecca and Jacob Motte: two sons and two daughters died young. It is possible that the second son listed by Salley as being born in 1764 and named Abraham was actually the son of Jacob's father. Motte Sr. remarried in 1763 and had a son named Abraham born in 1764. Sally lists the date of the first Mary's baptism as August 17, 1762, but her tombstone in St. Philip's Episcopal Church Cemetery says that she was born in September of 1761.

12. TP to Harriott Pinckney Horry (HPH), February 1775 in *The Papers of Eliza Lucas Pinckney*.

13. Sellers, *Charleston Business*, 192.

14. *Virginia Gazette* of December 1769 as quoted in *Becoming Americans Chronology 1754-1784* compiled by Cathéene Heiler and Nancy Milton.

15. Sellers, *Charleston Business*, 219-220.

16. "Charleston Non-Importation Agreement; July 22, 1769", Colonial Society of Massachusetts Publication, http://www.avalon.law.yale.edu/18th_century/charleston_non_impotation_1769.asp.

Chapter Four

1. Wallace, *South Carolina: A Short History*, 251-252.

2. ELP to HPH, March 1, 1775, in *The Papers of Eliza Lucas Pinckney*.

3. Ibid., ELP to HPH, March 9, 1775

4. *The South Carolina Gazette:* Wednesday, June 21st 1775. "In Provincial Congress Charles-Town, Wednesday, June 21st, 1775.

5. Smith and Smith, *The Dwelling Houses of Charleston*, 198.

6. *The South-Carolina Gazette*, January 30, 1775.

7. Elizabeth Trapier to HPH, 2 August 1775 in *The Papers of Eliza Lucas Pinckney*.

8. Bragg, *Crescent Moon Over Carolina*, 17.

9. https://www.carolana.com. See note 8 for 2nd Provincial Congress.

10. Ibid.

11. Gibbs, *Documentary History of the American Revolution*, 6-7.

12. Ibid., 7.

13. Richardson, *Standards and Colors of the American Revolution*, 132-134.

14. Bragg, *Crescent Moon Over Carolina*, p. 83-84.

15. Moultrie, *Memoirs of the American Revolution*, Vol. I, 183.

Chapter Five

1. Coquillette and York, *Portrait of a Patriot Volume 3, The Southern Journal*, 163.

2. Smith and Smith, *The Dwelling Houses of Charleston*, 198-199.

3. Mrs. Rebecca Motte to Charles Pinckney, Esquire and Frances his Wife, Renunciation of Inheritance, *Renunciation of Dower Book S136009 1775, Part I*, p 41-42. There is no corresponding Renunciation of Inheritance from Frances Pinckney to Rebecca Motte for the Mount Joseph Plantation that I could find, but Mount Joseph was owned by Rebecca Motte as she sold it to Elnathan Haskell in 1795.

4. South Carolina Wills and Probate Records for Miles Brewton, Vol 14-16, 1771-1779.

5. TP to HPH, February 1775. Pinckney Family Papers, Box 2, Folder 1, Library of Congress, Washington, DC.

6. TP to HPH 7 April 1778, in *The Papers of Eliza Lucas Pinckney*.

7. TP to HPH. June 4, 1778. Pinckney Family Papers, Box 2, Folder 1, Library of Congress, Washington, DC.

8. Williams, *A Founding Family*, 141, footnote 106.

9. Garden, Alexander, *Anecdotes of the American Revolution, Second Series*, 25.

Rebecca Brewton Motte

10. www.2ndsc.org/the-regiment-of-1775.html. The blue flag was taken by the British and was for many years at the museum of the 60th Regiment, the Kings Royal Rifle Corps at Winchester, England. It has since been returned and is on alternating display at the Smithsonian Institute in Washington, D. C. and the South Carolina State Museum in Columbia. The red flag was never recovered.

Chapter Six

1. Salley, "Col. Miles Brewton," 152.

2. TP to HPH 12 April 1780, in *The Papers of Eliza Lucas Pinckney*.

3. Tarleton, *A History of the Campaigns of 1780 and 1781 in the Southern Province of North America*, 27.

4. Ellet, *The Women of the American Revolution, Volume II*,.74.

5. Ravenel, *Eliza Pinckney*, viii.

6. Ibid., 287.

7. ELP to Elizabeth Motte Pinckney (EMP) 18 June 1780, in The Papers of Eliza Lucas Pinckney. At the end of her letter Eliza told Betsey that they had the pleasure of seeing her father at Hampton and that he was with them now. Therefore, he did not go to Mount Joseph with the rest of the family.

8. Ibid., EMP to ELP 17 July 1780.

9. Ibid., ELP to EMP, 18 June 1780.

10. Ibid., ELP to EMP, 18 June 1780.

11. Ibid., EMP to ELP 17 July 1780.

12. Ibid., EMP to ELP 17 July 1780.

13. Tarleton, *A History of the Campaigns of 1780 and 1781*, 75.

14. EMP to ELP 17 July 1780, in *The Papers of Eliza Lucas Pinckney*.

Chapter Seven

1. TP to Charles McGill, 29 August 1780, in *The Papers of Eliza Lucas Pinckney*.

2. Tarleton, *A History of the Campaign of 1780 and 1781*, 75.

3. TP to HPH 7 September 1780, in *The Papers of Eliza Lucas Pinckney.*

4. Ibid. TP to ELP 7 September 1780.

5. Ibid., TP to HPH 7 September 1780.

6. Ibid., TP to Horatio Gates, 18 August 1779.

7. Pinckney, *Life of General Thomas Pinckney by his grandson Rev. Charles Cotesworth Pinckney,* 77.

8. Banastre Tarleton to TP 2 September 1780, in *The Papers of Eliza Lucas Pinckney.*

9. John Money to T P, 24 September 1780, in *The Papers of the Revolutionary Era Pinckney Statesmen Digital Edition.*

10. Ibid., TP to John Money, 22 September 1780.

11. TP to HPH 26 September 1780 in *The Papers of Eliza Lucas Pinckney.*

12. Ibid., TP to HPH 26 September 1780.

13. Ibid., TP to Daniel (Charles Lucas Pinckney) Horry 26 October 1780.

14. Ibid., TP to Daniel (Charles Lucas Pinckney) Horry 26 October 1780.

15. Peter Manigault to Mrs. Manigault, 16 May 1753, in SCHGM, 32, 176.

16. CCP to ELP 1 December 1780, in *The Papers of Eliza Lucas Pinckney.*

17. Ibid., ELP to TP September 1780.

18. Ibid., ELP to TP 6 December 1780 and TP to ELP 6 December 1780.

19. Ibid., HPH to ELP 7 January 1781.

20. Ibid., ELP to TP 17 September 1780.

21. Ibid., HPH to ELP 7 January 1781.

22. Ibid., CCP to ELP 16 January 1781.

Chapter Eight

1. Kolb and Weir, ed., *Captured at Kings Mountain, the Journal of Uzal Johnson, a Loyalist Surgeon,* 17-18

2. McCrady, *The History of South Carolina in the Revolution, 1780-1783,* 232.

3. Garden, *Anecdotes,* 231.

4. Ibid., 232.

5. Ibid., 233.

6. Greene, *The Papers of Nathanael Greene Volume VI*, 589.

7. Sumter to Greene 7 April 1781, *The Papers of Nathanael Greene Volume VIII*, 67.

8. Smith et al., *"Obstinate and Strong," the History and Archaeology of the Siege of Fort Motte*, 21-22.

9. Garden, *Anecdotes*, 231.

10. Garden, *Anecdotes*, 231. Polly Brewton told Garden that the arrows had been given to Mr. Motte by a favorite African. It has been generally accepted that the arrows had been a gift to Miles Brewton. This story originated with Rebecca's grandson Charles Cotesworth Pinckney, II in a letter to the Columbia *Carolinian*, dated at Flat Rock September 27, 1855. Both Jacob Motte and Miles Brewton were merchants and were in a position to receive novelty gifts from captains of East India merchant ships. If the arrows had been a gift to Jacob Motte, it is more likely that Rebecca would have brought them with her from Fairfield than if they had been a gift to her brother. By the time C. C. Pinckney's account was written, Rebecca had been dead for forty years while Polly Brewton's account was given only two years after the Siege of Ft. Motte.

11. Ibid., 231. Polly calls McPherson a Major, but he is referred to as Lieutenant McPherson in Lord Rawdon's letter of condolences to him written May 14 and published in the *Royal Gazette* June 6, 1781.

12. Lee, *Memoirs*, 332.

13. McCrady, *The History of South Carolina*, 107-108.

14. Smith, Levi, Letter in *Royal Gazette*, April 17, 1782.

15. Smith, *"Obstinate and Strong,"* 23.

16. Ibid., 23.

17. Lee, *Memoirs*, 346-347.

18. Ibid., 346.

19. Ibid., 346.

20. Smith, *"Obstinate and Strong,"* 22.

21. Lee, *Memoirs*, 346.

American Patriot and Successful Rice Planter

22. Ibid., 347.

23. Harriot Rutledge to Charles Cotesworth Pinckney, October 9, 1855. *Charles C. Pinckney Family Papers, 1855-1945* (43/1096), South Carolina Historical Society, Charleston.

Chapter Nine

1. Harriott Rutledge to Charles C. Pinckney, October 9, 1855, *Charles C. Pinckney Family Papers, 1855-1945* (43/1096), South Carolina Historical Society, Charleston.

2. Ravenel, *Eliza Pinckney*, 300.

3. Smith, Thomas, *The Art of Gunnery*, London: 1643, p. 108 as quoted in "Two Revolutionary War Expedient Fire Arrows, 245.

4. Mackenzie, *Strictures*, p. 150-152 as quoted in "Two Revolutionary War Expedient Fire Arrows, From Archaeological Contexts in South Carolina" in *Military Collector & Historian, Vol. 71, No. 3*, 244-245.

5. Lee, *Memoirs*, 348.

6. Ibid. 348.

7. C.C. Pinckney, Letter to Columbia *Carolinian*, Flat Rock, 27 September 1855 as quoted in Salley, "Col. Miles Brewton," 149.

8. Garden, *Anecdotes*, 232.

9. C.C. Pinckney as quoted in Salley, "Col. Miles Brewton," 149.

10. General Orders, Headquarters, New Winsor, June 15, 1781 in John C. Fitzpatrick, ed *The Writings of George Washington, Volume 22 April 27, 1781-August 5, 1781*, 215-216.

11. Lee, *Memoirs*, 349.

12. Smith, Letter to *Royal Gazette*, April 17, 1782.

13. Ibid.

14. Ibid.

15. Ibid.

16. Ibid.

17. Ibid.

18. Ibid.

19. Lee, *Memoirs*, 348.

20. Pension application S9337. See Wayne Lynch, Facebook, May 30, 2020.

21. Gardner, *Anecdotes, 232.*

22. Ibid., 233.

23. Ibid., 233.

24. "The Letters of John Rutledge," *SCHGM, Vol 18, No. 4,* footnote p 155.

25. Gardner, *Anecdotes,* 232.

26. CCP to ELP July 25, 1781, in *The Papers of Eliza Lucas Pinckney.*

27. Buchannan, *Road to Charleston,* 216.

28. Ibid., 218.

29. Rutledge and Barnwell. "Letters of John Rutledge (Continued)." *SCHGM, Vol.18, No. 3,* 140.

30. Ibid., 139.

31. Letter, Pendleton to Simmons, November 9, 1781, in *Greene Papers, Volume IX,* 551.

Chapter Ten

1. Revolutionary War indent issued as payment for services rendered during the war to Rebecca Motte 1783. Records of the Comptroller General Accounts Audited for Revolutionary Service AA5383-A. South Carolina Department of Archives and History, Columbia, South Carolina.

2. Chastellux, *Travels in North America in the Years 1780-81-82,* 90.

3. TP to Nathanael Greene 31 March 1782, in *The Papers of the Revolutionary Era.* In his letter dated March 31st. Tom states that he had written to General Greene the previous Thursday about the capture of Pendleton the day before. In 1782 March 31st was on a Sunday which means that the capture took place on Wednesday the 27th.

4. Ibid.

5. Ibid., CCP to Arthur Middleton 24 April 1782.

6. Ibid. TP to Nathanael Greene 31 March 1782.

American Patriot and Successful Rice Planter

7. Ibid. CCP to Arthur Middleton 24 April 1782.

8. Ibid., TP to General Greene 31 March 1782.

9. Ibid., TP to Horatio Gates 17 June 1782.

10. "Correspondence of the Hon. Arthur Middleton," *SCHGM*, 3, 106-107.

11. Williams, *A Founding Family,* 186.

12. Gibbes, *Documentary History,* 179.

13. CP, II's body was later re-interred near the graves of his children in St. Philip's graveyard.

14. Barnwell, "The Evacuation of Charleston by the British in 1782," SCHGM vol. XI no.1, 15-16.

15. Ramsay, *History of South Carolina From Its First Settlement in 1670 to the Year 1808 Vol. II,* 384.

16. Barnwell, "The Evacuation", 15-16.

Chapter Eleven

1. Barnwell, "The Evacuation," 14.

2. Côté, Richard N., *Mary's World — Love, War and Family Ties in Nineteenth Century Charleston,* 79.

3. South Carolina Wills and Probate Records, 1670-1980 for Jacob Motte Sr. found on https://www.ancestrylibrary.com.

4. ELP to Mrs. Evance 25 Sept. 1780, in *The Papers of Eliza Lucas Pinckney.*

5. Ramsay, *History, Vol. II,* 430.

6. Court of Common Pleas; Writs of Partition 1777-1779; #13A.

7. Charleston Deed, Jacob Motte Sr. and Jr. to Miles Brewton and others, Trustees ST128 Book 3E pp 391-400 SC Department of Archives and History.

8. Rebecca Motte Administratrix of J. Motte vs Executors of William Garner. Court of Common Pleas, Judgment Rolls. Box 146A. NV 371A. Frs. 558-566 S7324.

9. Williams, *A Founding Family,* 198.

10. South Carolina Wills and Probate Records, 1670-1980 for Rebecca Motte, page 1005

Rebecca Brewton Motte

11. Ramsay, David to Commissioners of the Loan Office, Mortgage for One Town Lot on Tradd Street Charleston, Purchased from Frances Pinckney and Rebecca Motte (Plat and Appraisement) Date 4/2/1789. Series S218157, Volume 000B, Page 00392, Ignore 000, South Carolina Department of Archives and History, Columbia.

12. Sampson Neyle, by his executors, to Rebecca Motte, Lease and Release, 1784, Charleston County Register of Mesne Conveyance, Conveyance Books, 1776-1785, vol. 5KO, p. 358, South Carolina Department of Archives and History, Columbia.

13. TP to HPH 25 June 1789, in *The Papers of Eliza Lucas Pinckney*.

14. Heitzler. *Goose Creek: A Definitive History-Volume One Planters, Politicians And Patriots*, 200.

15. *Columbia Herald*, June 27, 1785.

16. HPH to ELP 7 and 8 November 1785, in *The Papers of Eliza Lucas Pinckney*.

17. CCP to TP 5 October 1794, in *The Papers of the Revolutionary Era*.

18. Walter Edgar, *South Carolina A History*, 246.

19. Chaplin, Joyce, Tidal Rice Cultivation and the Problem of Slavery in South Carolina and Georgia 1760-1815, *William & Mary Quarterly*, 40.

20. TP to ELP 16 September 1786, in *The Papers of Eliza Lucas Pinckney*.

21. Downey, "Lucas, Johnathan." *South Carolina Encyclopedia*, https://www.scencyclopedia.org/sce/entries/lucas-jonathan/

22. TP to HPH 19 August 1789, in *The Papers of Eliza Lucas Pinckney*.

23. South Carolina Wills and Probate Records for Rebecca Motte, 1670-1980, 1006.

24. TP to HPH 25 June 1789, in *The Papers of Eliza Lucas Pinckney*.

25. Ibid. TP to HPH 17 April 1790.

Chapter Twelve

1. Deed Book E-6, 507-510, Charleston County Register of Mesne Conveyances Office.

2. Côté, *Mary's World*, 32-33.

3. James Iredell to his wife (in Philadelphia from Charleston) 19 April 1792. *Life and Correspondence of James Iredell, Associate Justice of the U. S. Supreme Court, II,* 346.

4. There is documentation for only five children born to Betsey Motte Pinckney and Thomas Pinckney — two boys and three girls. However, in a letter to her sister Mary dated 3 October 1792, Betsey wrote: "I shall take Becky with me and leave Cotesworth (Charles Cotesworth Pinckney, II) with Mrs. Keiffe, the other four are at School. Tom (Thomas Pinckney Jr.) at Westminster, the girls at Chelsea." This makes six children. In another letter to Mary dated 4 August 1792 Betsey chides her sister for not writing to her, but excuses her "as I know the employment of six Children by experience." It is apparent that Betsey had six children — the two boys mentioned above and four girls: Elizabeth Brewton Pinckney, Harriott Lucas Pinckney, Rebecca Motte Pinckney and one daughter for whom I could find no record.

5. EMP to RBM 3 October 1792, in *The Papers of the Revolutionary Era.*

6. Ibid. EMP to Mary Brewton Motte Alston, 16 August 1792.

7. CCP to TP 4 February 1794, in *The Papers of Eliza Lucas Pinckney.*

8. CCP to TP 13 September 1794, in *The Papers of the Revolutionary Era.*

9. Ibid., CCP to TP 4 November 1794.

10. Ibid., TP to Edward Rutledge 22 August 1794.

11. Ibid., CCP to TP 4 November 1794.

12. Alice Delancey Izard to Ralph Izard 4 December 1794, in *The Papers of Eliza Lucas Pinckney.*

13. CCP to TP 5 October 1794, in *The Papers of the Revolutionary Era.*

14. Ibid., CCP to TP 5 October 1794.

15. Ibid., CCP to TP 4 November 1794.

16. "Marriage and Death Notices" reprinted from the *City Gazette* in SCHGM Volume XXIII (1922) p. 30.

17. TP to Frances Motte Middleton Pinckney 1 August 1796, in *The Papers of the Revolutionary Era.*

18. September 1-2, 1795 Conveyance by Rebecca Motte to Elnathan Haskell. Charleston Deeds Vol. Q-6, 67-71.

19. There is no record of when Rebecca sold Motte's Wharf. She simply mentioned in her will that she had sold it with her daughters' permission to Mr. William Crafts. It is highly likely that since it was commercial property, it would have been easier to sell in the years right after the war than a plantation and therefore, was the first of her holdings that she sold.

20. Thomas and Frances Motte Middleton Pinckney, Charleston County Probate Court, Will Book 38, 571-582.

21. Stoney, *Plantations of the Carolina Low Country*,73. The house at Eldorado burned in 1897 and only the ruins remain.

22. Leiding, *Historic Houses of South Carolina*, 104.

23. Elizabeth Brewton Pinckney to TP 17 April 1798, in *The Papers of the Revolutionary Era*.

24. Ibid., Elizabeth Brewton Pinckney to TP, 17 April 1798.

25. RBM to Mary Motte Alston, 1806 in *Alston, Pringle, Frost Papers (28/630/2)* South Carolina Historical Society.

26. Ibid., RBM to Mary Alston 6 February 1807.

27. TP to HPH 24 and 26 February 1809 in *The Papers of Eliza Lucas Pinckney*.

28. Thomas and Frances Motte Middleton Pinckney, Charleston County Probate Court, Will Book 38,571-582. Tom and Fanny mention in their joint will that Charles Cotesworth helped his grandmother manage her estate at Eldorado.

29. South Carolina Wills and Probate Records, 1670-1980, for Rebecca Motte, page 1005.

Epilogue

1. Ellet, *Women of the American Revolution*, x.

2. Ibid., 77.

3. Ibid., 75.

4. Ibid., 74.

5. Ibid., 77.

Addendum, Fort Motte — Then and Now

1. Lossing, *The Pictorial Field Book of the Revolution*, 477.

2. Smith, *"Obstinate and Strong,"* 9.

3. James Jamieson to Freedmen's Bureau, March 2, 1868 in South Carolina Freedmen's Bureau Field Office Records, 1865-1872, roll 69, image 105-107.

4. Orangeburg County Deed Book 8, 289.

5. Smith, *"Obstinate and Strong,"* 11.

6. Lee, *Memoirs*, 348.

7. Smith, *"Obstinate and Strong,"* 11.

8. Harriott Pinckney Horry Rutledge to Charles Cotesworth Pinckney, October 9, 1855 *Charles C. Pinckney Family Papers, 1855-1945*, (43/1096) South Carolina Historical Society, Charleston.

9. Smith, *"Obstinate and Strong,"* 11.

Bibliography

Bailey, Louise N., ed. *Biographical Dictionary of the South Carolina Senate.* Columbia: University of South Carolina Press, 1986.

Barnwell, Joseph W. "The Evacuation of Charleston by the British in 1782." *South Carolina History and Genealogical Magazine Vol XI, No. 1.*

Borick, Carl P. *A Gallant Defense the Siege of Charleston, 1780.* Columbia: University of South Carolina Press, 2003.

_____. *Relieve Us of This Burthen, American Prisoners of War in the Revolutionary South, 1780 – 1782.* Columbia: University of South Carolina Press, 2012.

Brag, C. L. *Crescent Moon over Carolina William Moultrie & American Liberty.* Columbia: University of South Carolina Press, 2013.

Bridges, Anne Baker Leland and Williams, Roy, III. *St. James Santee Plantation Parish, History And Records 1685-1925.* Spartanburg: The Reprint Company, Publishers, 1997.

Broad, John. "Cattle Plague in 18th-Century England," *British Agricultural History Review* Vol 31, No. 2, 1983.

Chaplin, Joyce E. "Tidal Rice Cultivation and the Problem of Slavery in South Carolina and Georgia, 1760-1815," *William and Mary Quarterly,* No. 1, 1992.

Chastellux, François-Jean Marquis de. *Travels in North America in the Years 1780-81-82.* New York: np, 1828.

Conrad, Dennis, ed. *The Papers of Nathanael Greene, Volume VIII.* Chapel Hill: University of North Carolina Press, 1995.

Côté, Richard N. *Mary's World – Love, War, and Family Ties in Nineteenth Century Charleston.* Mount Pleasant, South Carolina: Corinthian Books, 2001.

Coquillette, Daniel R. & York, Neil Longley, ed. *Portrait of a Patriot, Volume Three, the Southern Journal.* Boston: The Colonial Society of Massachusetts, 2007.

David, Huw. *Trade, Politics and Revolution: South Carolina and Britain's Atlantic Commerce 1730-1790.* Columbia: University of South Carolina Press: 2018.

Earle, Peter. *The Making of the English Middle Class: Business, Society and Family Life In London, 1660-1730.* Berkley: University of California Press, 1989.

Edgar, Walter B., ed. and N. Louise Bailey. *Biographical Directory of the South Carolina House of Representatives, Volume II, The Commons House of Assembly, 1692-1775.* Columbia: University of South Carolina Press, 1986.

Edgar, Walter B. *South Carolina A History.* Columbia: University of South Carolina Press, 1998.

Ellet, Elizabeth F. *Women of the American Revolution, Volume Two.* New York: Baker and Scribner, 1849.

Fitzpatrick, John C. ed. *The Writings of George Washington, Volume 22 April 27-August 5,1781.* Washington, D. C.: U. S. Printing Office, 1931.

Garden, Alexander. *Anecdotes of the revolutionary war in America: with sketches of character of persons the most distinguished, in the Southern states, for civil and military service.* Charleston, SC: A. E Miller, 1822.

Gibbes, Robert W. *Documentary History of the American Revolution, Vol. 3.* New York: D. Appleton & Co., 1857.

Green, Nathanael. *The Papers of General Nathanael Greene, Volume IX.* Providence: Rhode Island Historical Society, 1989.

Harrison, Margaret Hayne. *A Charleston Album.* Rindge, New Hampshire: Richard R. Smith Publisher, Inc., 1953.

Heiler, Cathéene and Nancy Milton. *Becoming Americans Chronology 1754-1784.* Williamsburg, VA: Colonial Williamsburg Foundation, 1996.

Heitzler, Michael J. *Goose Creek: A Definitive History-Volume One: Planters, Politicians and Patriots.* Charleston: History Press, 2005.

Hopkins, Donald R. *The Greatest Killer: Smallpox in History.* Chicago: University of Chicago Press, 2002.

Hotten, John Camden, ed. *List of People Who Went From Great Britain to the American Plantations 1600-1700.* New York: G. A. Baker and Co., Inc., 1931.

Kolb, Wade S., III, ed. and Robert M. Weir. *Captured at Kings Mountain, The Journal of Uzal Johnson, a Loyalist Surgeon.* Columbia: University of South Carolina Press, 2011.

Krawcznski, Keith. "Smith, Benjamin," *South Carolina Encyclopedia.* www.scencyclopedia.org/sce/entries/smith-benjamin/.

Leiding, Harriette Kershaw. *Historic Houses of South Carolina.* Philadelphia: J. B. Lippencott Company, 1921.

Lossing, Benson. *The Pictorial Field-book of the Revolution.* New York: Harper and Brothers, 1860.

McCrady, Edward. *The History of South Carolina in the Revolution, 1780-1783.* New York: Russell and Russell, 1902.

McRee, Griffith J. *Life and Correspondence of James Iredell, Associate Justice of the U. S. Supreme Court, II.* New York: Appleton and Company, 1857.

Moultrie, William. *Memoirs of the American Revolution: so far as it related to the states of North and South Carolina and Georgia.* New York: D. Longworth, 1802.

Oller, John. *The Swamp Fox: How Francis Marion Saved the American Revolution.* Boston: Da Capo Press, 2016.

Pringle, Elizabeth W. Allston. *A Woman Rice Planter.* New York: Macmillan Company, 1913.

Ramsay, David. *History of South Carolina From Its First Settlement in 1670 to the Year 1808, Vol. 2.* Charleston: David Longworth, 1809.

Ravenel, Harriott Horry. *Eliza Pinckney.* New York: Charles Scribner's Sons, 1896.

Richardson, Edward W. *Standards and Colors of the American Revolution.* Philadelphia: University of Pennsylvania Press, 1982.

Rogers, George C. Jr. *Charleston in the Age of the Pinckneys.* Columbia: University of South Carolina Press, 1980.

_____, *The History of Georgetown County, South Carolina.* Columbia: University of South Carolina Press, 1970.

Russell, David Lee. "Life in the Southern Colonies," *Journal of the American Revolution.* www.allthingsliberty.com/2013/life-in-the-southern-colonies-part-1-of-3/.

Salley, A. S. Jr. "Col. Miles Brewton and Some of His Descendants," *South Carolina Historical and Genealogical Magazine Vol.2, No. 2.*

Schulz, Constance, ed. *The Papers of Eliza Lucas Pinckney and Harriott Pinckney Horry Digital Edition* (American Founding Era Collection). Charlottesville: University of Virginia Press Rotunda, 2012.

_____. *The Papers of the Revolutionary Era Pinckney Statesmen Digital Edition,* ed. Constance B. Schulz. Charlottesville: University of Virginia Press, Rotunda, 2016.

Sellers, Leila. *Charleston Business on the Eve of the American Revolution.* Chapel Hill: University of North Carolina Press, 1934.

Smith, Alice R. Huger, and D. E. Huger Smith. *Dwelling Houses of Charleston, SouthCarolina.* Charleston: History Press, 2007.

Smith, Levi. Letter to *Royal Gazette,* April 17, 1782.

Smith, Steven, James Legg, Tamara Wilson, and Johnathan Leader. *"Obstinate and Strong": The History and Archaeology of the Siege of Ft. Motte,* Columbia: University ofSouth Carolina — South Carolina Institute of Archaeology and Anthropology, 2007.

Smith et.al. "Two Revolutionary War Expedient Fire Arrows from Archaeological ContextsIn South Carolina," *Military Collector and Historian Magazine, Vol.71, No. 3, Fall 2019.*

Stoney, Samuel Gaillard. *Plantations of the Carolina Low Country,* New York: Dover Publications, Inc., 1989 edition.

Webber, Mabel L., "The Register of Christ Church Parish," *SCHGM, XXI, No. 1.*

Wehle, Harry B. and Theodore Bolton. *American Miniatures 1730-1850,* New York: Garden City Publishing Company, 1937.

Weir, Robert. *Colonial South Carolina, a History,* Columbia: University of South Carolina Press, 1997.

Wister, Mrs. O. J. and Miss Agnes Irwin. *Worthy Women of Our First Century,* Philadelphia: J. B. Lippencott Co. 1877.

Williams, Frances Leigh. *A Founding Family, The Pinckneys of South Carolina,* New York: Harcourt Brace Jovanovich, 1978.

Index

A
Alston, Mary Motte (Mrs. William) 12, 149-152, 164; *see also* Motte, Mary
Alston, William 149

B
Belleville Plantation 86, 89, 92-93, 97-100, 115-116, 158
Brewton, Frances 5, 7, 10-11; *see also* Pinckney, Frances Brewton
Brewton, Mary Griffith Loughton (Mrs. Robert) 1, 5, 8-9
Brewton, Mary (Polly) (Mrs. John) 62, 86-87, 89-90, 93, 100, 104, 111-113
Brewton, Miles (1675-1745) 1-4, 6
Brewton, Miles (1731-1775) 5, 7, 39-40, 42-44, 50-51, 71
Brewton, Robert (1698-1759) 1, 4-6, 9, 17-18, 22

C
Camden 70-71, 73, 82-83, 85-86, 96, 112, 114-116; battle of 77-80
Charles Town(e) 2, 54, 67; *see also* Charleston
Charleston 2-7, 10, 15-16, 18-20, 22-23, 25, 28-31, 35-39, 41, 43-45, 48, 134-136, 138, 142, 146-148, 159, 161-165; British occupation of 62-65, 67-68, 71-73, 76-78, 82, 84-89, 97, 111-113, 117-121, 123, 125-126, 128-133; *see also* Charles Town(e)
Clinton, Sir Henry 44, 47, 60-61, 65, 74-75
Cornwallis, Charles Lord 44, 65-66, 69-71, 74, 78, 90-92, 118, 128

D
Dart, Martha Motte (Mrs. John Sanford) 62, 75, 83

E
Eldorado Plantation 141, 146, 148, 152-154, 160-165,
Ellet, Elizabeth vii, xii-xiii, 67, 167-170, 172
Elliott, Bernard 41, 43, 46-47, 49
Elliott, Susannah Smith (Mrs. Bernard) 41, 45-48, 59; *see also* Smith, Susannah
Eutaw Springs 116-118

F
Fairfield Plantation 22, 28, 31, 37, 42, 45, 62-64, 66-69, 72, 118-119, 121-126, 137, 140-142, 147-148, 153, 155, 159-163
Fort Motte 67, 93, 95, 97-99, 104-106, 110-112, 135, 167, 170-174; town of 170, 172
Fort Watson 86, 95-96,

G
Gates, Gen. Horatio 77-79, 81, 90
Greene, Gen. Nathanael 90-97, 101, 109-112, 114-118, 120-126, 129-130, 132, 136

H
Hampton Plantation 31, 62-63, 66-68, 121, 123-125, 142, 148, 150
Horry, Daniel 31, 66-68, 87, 103, 130-131, 142,
Horry, Harriott Pinckney 31, 40, 53-54, 62, 84, 86-87, 103, 131, 142-143, 145-146, 150, 152-153, 161, 163-164

L
Lee, Lt. Col. Henry 94-106, 108-112, 173
Lincoln, General Benjamin 55-59, 63-64
Lucas, Jonathan 146-147, 163

M
Marion, Francis 59, 77-78, 85, 94-103, 105, 107-112, 121, 130, 173,
McKenzie, Captain Charles Barrington 79-80
McPherson, Lieutenant 89-90, 93, 98, 100, 104-106, 108, 111, 173
Middleton, Frances Motte (Mrs. John) 138, 141-143, 145-147, 152-157, 159-160; *see also* Motte, Frances; Pinckney, Frances Motte Middleton
Middleton, John 100, 135, 137, 140-142, 174
Miles Brewton House 50-51, 64, 134, 140, 149
Motte, Charles 38, 46, 60
Motte, Elizabeth (Betsey) 24, 53-54, 57; *see also* Pinckney, Betsey Motte
Motte, Frances (Fanny) 24, 62, 100, 135, 137, 174; *see also* Middleton, Frances Motte; Pinckney, Frances Motte Middleton
Motte, Isaac 21, 25-26, 38, 42, 46, 48

Motte, Jacob, Jr. 13, 15-26, 28-30, 34-35, 37-39, 51-52, 57, 63, 66, 68-69, 72, 81-82, 84-88, 93, 136-140

Motte, Jacob, Sr. 14-21, 34, 138

Motte, Mary 30, 62, 75, 100, 149; *see also* Alston, Mary Motte

Motte's Wharf 16-17, 19, 138-139, 165

Mount Joseph plantation 51, 67, 69, 71-73, 75, 80-83, 85-89, 92, 111, 115-118, 138-139, 158

Musket arrows 103-105

P

Pendleton, Henry 122-126

Pinckney, Charles, II (1730-1782) 10-11, 63, 127-129, 131

Pinckney, Charles Cotesworth (1746-1825) 67, 113-114, 129, 148, 153-56

Pinckney, Charles Cotesworth, II (Cotesworth, 1789-1865) 159, 165

Pinckney, Eliza Lucas 12, 67, 72-73, 75, 84, 86-87, 123, 136-137, 143, 151

Pinckney, Betsey (Mrs. Thomas) 62, 72-75, 80, 83-84, 90, 113, 119, 121-123, 137-138, 145, 151-152, 154, 157; *see also* Motte, Elizabeth (Betsey)

Pinckney, Frances Brewton (Mrs. Charles) 40, 43-44, 50-51, 127, 130, 139-140, 149, 155-156, *see also* Brewton, Frances

Pinckney, Frances Motte Middleton (Mrs. Thomas) 161-164; *see also* Motte, Frances; Middleton, Frances Motte

Pinckney, Thomas 13, 53, 57-58, 62-64, 66-68, 72-73, 77, 79-85, 90, 113, 121-126, 137-138, 143, 145-147, 150-151, 153, 155-165

R

Rawdon, Francis Lord 78, 92, 94, 98, 100-101, 104, 110, 112, 114-115

Rice cultivation 143-147

Rutledge, Gov. John 36, 44, 49, 63-65, 69-70, 72, 114-117, 120, 161

S

Sampson 72, 75, 81,

Savannah Second Battle of 58-60

Smith, Levi 98, 106-109

Smith, Stephen D. 172-174

Smith, Susannah 24, 37-38, 41; *see also* Elliott, Susannah Smith

Sumter, Thomas 76-78, 92, 96, 98, 110

T

Tarleton, Lt. Col. Banastre 66, 69-71, 81

Thomson, William 45, 89, 92, 97-98, 105, 158

W

Wannamaker, Luther 171

Washington, George 72, 147, 149-150, 157-158